THE PSYCHOLOGY OF HAPPINESS

Is happiness all down to luck? Do events in our life influence how happy we feel? Can too much of a good thing make us less happy?

The Psychology of Happiness introduces readers to the variety of factors that can affect how happy we are. From our personality and feelings of self-worth, to our physical health and employment status, happiness is a subjective experience which will change throughout our lives. Although feeling happy is linked with positive thinking and our sociability in daily life, the book also includes surprising facts about the limitations of our personal happiness.

We all want to feel happy in our lives, and *The Psychology of Happiness* shows us that achieving it can be both an accident of fortune and a direct result of our own actions and influence.

Peter Warr is Emeritus Professor of Psychology at the University of Sheffield, UK.

D1190817

THE PSYCHOLOGY OF EVERYTHING

People are fascinated by psychology, and what makes humans tick. Why do we think and behave the way we do? We've all met armchair psychologists claiming to have the answers, and people that ask if psychologists can tell what they're thinking. The Psychology of Everything is a series of books which debunk the popular myths and pseudo-science surrounding some of life's biggest questions.

The series explores the hidden psychological factors that drive us, from our subconscious desires and aversions, to our natural social instincts. Absorbing, informative, and always intriguing, each book is written by an expert in the field, examining how research-based knowledge compares with popular wisdom, and showing how psychology can truly enrich our understanding of modern life.

Applying a psychological lens to an array of topics and contemporary concerns – from sex, to fashion, to conspiracy theories – The Psychology of Everything will make you look at everything in a new way.

For further information about this series please visit
www.thepsychologyofeverything.co.uk

THE PSYCHOLOGY OF HAPPINESS

PETER WARR

Routledge
Taylor & Francis Group

LONDON AND NEW YORK

First published 2019
by Routledge
2 Park Square, Milton Park, Abingdon, Oxon OX14 4RN

and by Routledge
711 Third Avenue, New York, NY 10017

Routledge is an imprint of the Taylor & Francis Group, an informa business

British Library Cataloguing-in-Publication Data
A catalogue record for this book is available from the British Library

Library of Congress Cataloging-in-Publication Data
Names: Warr, Peter B., author.
Title: The Psychology of Happiness / by Peter Warr.
Description: 1 Edition. | New York : Routledge, 2019. |
    Includes bibliographical references and index.
Identifiers: LCCN 2018057598 | ISBN 9781138090668 (hardback)
Subjects: LCSH: Happiness.
Classification: LCC BF575.H27 W367 2019 | DDC 152.4/2—dc23
LC record available at https://lccn.loc.gov/2018057598

ISBN: 978-1-138-09066-8 (hbk)
ISBN: 978-1-138-09079-8 (pbk)
ISBN: 978-1-315-10845-2 (ebk)

Typeset in Joanna
by Apex CoVantage, LLC

CONTENTS

PREFACE

Almost everyone is concerned about happiness – their own or other people's. What is it, what affects it, and what does it lead to? In many cases, its opposite is the concern – unhappiness or distress.

As a university researcher, I have for several decades carried out studies in this area, often described in terms of 'wellbeing', and I've published many papers and books for academic readers. In addition, I've long felt it important that academic thinking and findings should be made available to a wider public. With that in mind, I worked with journalist Guy Clapperton to publish *The Joy of Work?* in 2010, and the five different editions of *Psychology at Work* between 1971 and 2002 were addressed to nonacademic readers as well as to students and their teachers.

Writing about research for people outside the academic bubble requires books that are inexpensive enough to attract casual readers. And that means they have to be short. This series (*The Psychology of Everything* by publishers Routledge) requires authors to stay within a fixed word limit in order to allow a low selling price. It provides easy-to-read introductions for general readers and for professionals and students in a book's area, aiming to spread academic thinking outside universities.

The series is thus ideal for communicating research to people at large. This book aims to do that. It explores the causes, characteristics and consequences of happiness and unhappiness in a relaxed manner, complementing academics' more formal style. Some readers will be students of psychology and related subjects; for them and for possible use by researchers from other fields, a number of academic publications are cited by means of notes throughout the text and are listed at the end of the book. Please note that the content does not directly concern mental illness and therapy.

As a limited-length overview of research into happiness, the chapters that follow take a broad-brush approach. That contrasts with individual research investigations that necessarily focus on particular frameworks and localized issues. Of course, the two levels of specificity complement each other, and many detailed findings and models can be placed within the present comprehensive account.

This book has evolved over several years, and I am indebted to a large number of people. I thank the researchers in many countries who have laid the foundations of my own thinking, and I am particularly grateful to colleagues at the University of Sheffield in the Institute of Work Psychology and previously in the MRC/ESRC Social and Applied Psychology Unit. Many thanks to everyone.

Peter Warr
Sheffield, UK

1

AN INITIAL LOOK

Happiness and unhappiness are central to our existence. Their dependence on personal desires and motives means that in some form they underpin almost every thought and action, and surveys across the world have found that happiness is considered to be the most important aspect of life. Similarly, happiness is at the heart of psychology. Many psychological themes – as in attitudes, habits, motivation, reinforcement, personality traits, values, preferences and prejudices – reflect happiness-related feelings[1] in one form or another, although academic and other presentations may not mention happiness at all. Instead the explicit references are to enjoyment, desire, preference, want, need and interest or to distress, anxiety, depression and despair – all illustrating aspects of happiness and unhappiness. Many other meanings will be reviewed throughout the book.[2]

Definitions are fairly straightforward in outline terms, but as so often the devil is in the detail. We'll be looking at people who have 'a deep sense of pleasure or contentment' (from the Oxford English Dictionary) or are 'characterized by pleasure, contentment or joy' (from Dictionary.com). We'll also be examining negative feelings of unhappiness, strain and distress, and we will need to check beyond merely feeling good or feeling bad to include more elusive notions of 'flourishing'.

Details of definition and measurement are covered in Chapters 2 and 3. At this outline stage, we should recognize another central theme in dictionary definitions, the possession of good luck. Dictionary.com also tells us that happy people are those who are 'favored by fortune; fortunate or lucky'. Indeed happiness-as-luck was historically the term's primary definition. The word is based on early-English *hap*, and words like *happenstance*, *mishap* and *hapless* have retained *hap* as their stem. 'Good hap' was offered in Middle Ages England rather than 'good luck', and many countries still use fortune, fate or luck as the construct's primary meaning. Good fortune is in 80 per cent of current dictionary definitions of happiness across the world.[3]

Fortunate coincidences are certainly important for happiness. Were you lucky enough to be born with the right genes? Did your chance genetic makeup come from parents who turned out to be supportive? Did happenings in your life come together positively instead of fate conspiring against you? Did the many people you met turn out to include a future partner? When it came to jobs, were you coincidentally in the right place at the right time? In terms of bad luck, did a car driver unexpectedly swerve in front of you? So much depends on how your cards fall.[4]

Only around a century ago did Western countries shift the meaning of happiness to prioritize positive feeling states, and the construct became principally defined in terms of pleasant experiences rather than, as for hundreds of years, in terms of benevolent fate or good fortune. Despite a general similarity between Eastern and Western uses of the term, Japanese and Chinese notions of happiness particularly emphasize social harmony and group welfare, whereas Americans are more concerned with personal goal-attainment.[5]

Even within a single culture, people can have different views. For example, research has looked at the meaning of happiness for people at different ages. Analyses within the United States of personal blogs and findings from surveys and laboratory studies have pointed to differences between the teenage years and several decades later. Whereas young people are likely to associate happiness with excitement and fun, older ones see it more in terms of peacefulness and the avoidance of stress.[6]

In general, there is a small bias to positive: people overall tend to be slightly happy rather than unhappy. And in almost every case, happiness has a target. We are 'happy with' or 'happy about' something – an object, idea, person, group or ourselves.[7] American psychologist Charles Osgood showed that positive or negative evaluation is involved in almost every experience. Together with colleagues, he explored the 'connotative' meaning of thousands of words – what the words imply to people beyond their dictionary ('denotative') meaning. From many studies around the world, it was clear that a large factor of evaluation, from dislike to like, is primary within the connotative meaning of any word, irrespective of what it denotes.[8] Evaluations – feelings of positivity or negativity – are central to our thinking about almost everything, even though denotative meaning may conceal that fact.

HAPPINESS AND WELLBEING

Given that happiness or unhappiness is almost always directed at something or somebody, it's important to distinguish between targets' different levels of scope. Let's think in terms of three levels: expanding from (the narrowest) 'feature-specific' happiness through 'domain-specific' happiness on to wide-ranging 'global' or 'context-free' happiness. *Feature-specific* happiness or unhappiness is experienced in the continuous stream of likes or dislikes that occur throughout life – positive or negative feelings about a single thing, person, idea or activity. These feelings are not necessarily experienced in terms of 'being happy' or 'being unhappy'. You might feel enthusiastic, excited, calm, relaxed, gloomy, anxious or in many other ways to be reviewed later, but those feelings all represent happiness.

At the second level of scope, with a medium-range focus beyond single features, is *domain-specific* happiness or unhappiness. That's concerned with feelings in a particular segment of life – about *sets of* things, people, ideas or activities. At this middle breadth of scope, we might study feelings about a particular area of life, for example, asking people about happiness with their job or their health or about a category of people (family members, work colleagues, etc.) or a set of ideas (e.g., a particular religious ideology). This middle-scope level of happiness includes prejudices directed at the generality of people from a certain country, race, gender, age and so on.

Third, the broadest form of happiness (global or *context-free*) covers feelings about your life as a whole. How positive do you feel in general when considering all aspects of your life? With this wide scope, we might study life satisfaction, overall happiness or generalized anxiety. Context-free happiness is usually what writers have in mind when comparing particular groups or countries, often citing national differences based on overall satisfaction with life.

Happiness at this global, context-free level largely derives from the accumulation of localized experiences that are themselves restricted to single features or single domains. Different instances of narrow-scope happiness combine across time to generate more wide-ranging feelings about your life. Focussed forms of happiness are the building blocks of life satisfaction and other examples of global wellbeing, so feature-specific and domain-specific instances are central to this book.[9]

Types and measures of wellbeing

The term 'wellbeing' is frequently used as synonymous with happiness and is particularly favoured by academic researchers.[10] The two words have often been treated as largely interchangeable, but we should note that wellbeing is a broader notion than happiness itself. Wellbeing as a whole extends beyond the subjective experiences in happiness to also cover wellbeing that is physical, social, economic or spiritual. Given that our focus is on *subjective* or *psychological* wellbeing, otherwise viewed as happiness, the other kinds of wellbeing will receive only limited attention here.

Within psychological wellbeing, we should distinguish between forms that are 'hedonic' and those concerned with 'flourishing'. The term 'hedonic' derives from the Greek word for pleasure (*hēdon*), and a hedonic perspective on happiness is in terms of experienced pleasure and pain, such that happy people experience more positive feelings than negative ones.[11] In those terms, happiness or unhappiness about targets of a particular scope can be measured through positive or negative feelings. And yet there's more to hedonic happiness and unhappiness than merely positivity or negativity; feelings also vary in their activation or arousal. Positive wellbeing includes, for instance, not only joyful cheerfulness (activated as well as positive) but also contented peace of mind (positive but low activation). Similarly, negative feelings can be tense and anxious (high activation) or sad and depressed (low activation). These different kinds of experience will be explored in Chapter 2.

In contrast to the focus on feelings within hedonic wellbeing, 'flourishing' wellbeing emphasizes aspects of personal functioning. Drawing on Aristotle's (384–322 BC) philosophical discussions of *eudaimonia* – a good, worthwhile or fulfilled life – the construct has in recent years been developed and modified by psychologists. Researchers have viewed it in different ways, and psychologists have debated its definition and contents within happiness without reaching complete consensus.[12] In general, flourishing involves undertaking activity that is somehow worthwhile or valued or can contribute to attaining one's 'true self'.

As we'll see in Chapter 3, writers have emphasized involvement in issues beyond oneself, building up self-worth, working towards valued objectives, becoming psychologically immersed in an activity, contributing to others, and personal thriving and development. Flourishing wellbeing has in these ways been viewed as the achievement of personal meaning in life and working towards self-realization or self-validation – notions that have much in common with earlier ideas about self-actualization and psychological growth.[13]

The time focus of experienced happiness depends on how you direct your attention. For both hedonic and flourishing wellbeing, studies of happiness can be directed at time periods of any duration, from 'this very minute' through 'this afternoon', 'this week' and 'this month', and extending to 'my life as a whole'. In addition, an across-time perspective has asked about 'me as a person', through a dispositional indicator that is often referred to as 'trait happiness' in contrast to more short-term forms of 'state happiness'. Importantly, longer-term wellbeing is largely based on earlier short-term feelings about particular situations.

For assessing different forms of wellbeing, psychologists have developed a wide range of self-description questionnaires and interview schedules. On the one hand, information might be gathered about people's recollection of happiness in an earlier period (asking about happiness or related experiences across 'the last month', in 'your life as a whole' and so on), or alternatively the focus can be on a current or very recent situation, for example, by requesting experiences at this particular moment in response to randomly timed cues from small electronic alarms. Retrospective self-reports of previous or general feelings are easier for both investigators and research participants, but they can suffer from errors of recall,[14] whereas sampling very recent experiences yields potentially more accurate information but is open to concerns about generality: are these recent or current experiences typical for the person across a longer period?

In all empirical research, we are in effect applying an *operational* definition; the variable is being defined in terms of the measure applied – its operationalization. However, that operational definition may well or poorly represent an underlying *conceptual* definition – the inherent meaning of the construct. Since different operationalizations are often possible for the same concept and many have been used for happiness, different researchers' investigations may in fact be addressing several versions of the same concept. That situation can be acceptable, but it does mean that we must check carefully how a variable has been defined conceptually and how well that conceptual definition has been operationalized in a particular study or discussion; different operationalizations can be measuring different concepts despite using the same concept-name.

Happiness and unhappiness sometimes occur in feelings that overall are ambivalent – mixing positive and negative, as people feel happy and unhappy about different aspects. Ambivalence can also occur across time, as progress in personal projects may require working through obstacles or struggling with limited resources before progress is made and success is achieved; in those cases, you have to feel bad before you can feel good.

That kind of interdependence between opposites is particularly emphasized in Chinese notions of 'yin' and 'yang' (the 'dark side' and the 'bright side'), such that everything in the world is seen as having two aspects that are both complementary and contrasting. Yin and yang are seen as interdependent, and each is inseparably present within the other; everything is a balanced mixture of them both.

As we'll see later, hedonic wellbeing has been more precisely conceptualized and operationalized than has flourishing and has been investigated in more detail. For much of the world's population, reducing hedonic unhappiness may be more important than experiencing a sense of flourishing; self-actualization can seem an unrealistic goal when you're struggling to cope with a mountain of problems and need to reduce your own and your family's distress.

Collectively, those two kinds of happiness have much in common with the notion of mental health. That is itself difficult to define, but one general overview suggests that positive mental health might be described as a combination of subjective wellbeing, competence, aspiration, autonomy and specific forms of integrated functioning.[15] The first of those elements – subjective wellbeing – is similar to hedonic wellbeing as considered here, and the other four components – competence, aspiration, autonomy and integrated functioning – overlap with aspects of flourishing.

Finally in this introduction, we should distinguish sharply between happiness and its possible causes. Many writers have mixed them up. 'Happiness is a good meal' or 'happiness is relaxing in the sunshine' can make for an entertaining magazine article, but of course the good meal or relaxing in the sunshine are not part of happiness; they are possible causes of the experience and not the experience itself. This book will retain that separation between happiness and its causes, examining the construct itself in Chapters 2 and 3 and reviewing the causes of happiness in Chapters 4 and 5. Possible consequences will be explored in Chapter 6 before the final chapter considers what we might do next.

CHAPTER 1: SOME TAKE-HOME MESSAGES

Happiness almost always has a target (we're 'happy about' or 'happy with' something or somebody), and happiness experiences take many different forms that are often described without referring to 'happiness' itself. Instead we're said to be 'enjoying' or 'liking' something or finding it 'attractive', 'intriguing', 'amusing' or similar. It's particularly important to specify which level of scope (feature-specific, domain-specific or context-free) is being considered, and daily life often yields a stream of localized happiness experiences that can together contribute to overall life satisfaction. Happiness and unhappiness can coexist or follow each other, and a 'happy person' may be thought of in both hedonic and flourishing terms.

2

HEDONIC WELLBEING
Feeling bad to feeling good

Let's now look in more detail at the two kinds of happiness. This chapter will consider hedonic wellbeing, and in Chapter 3 we'll turn to the characteristics and possible measures of flourishing. First, we should note that researchers have explored hedonic wellbeing in two ways, either through compound scales of feelings and associated thoughts or by asking directly about feelings alone. Let's consider those two in turn.

HEDONIC MEASURES (1): COMPOUNDS OF THOUGHT AND FEELING

Cognitive-affective[1] compounds mix together feelings with ideas, recollections, perspectives and mental networks, and happiness or unhappiness composites have been examined through multi-item scales of life satisfaction, overall happiness, engagement, strain, depression, burnout and so on. For instance, at the context-free level of scope, the established Satisfaction with Life scale includes 'In most ways my life is close to my ideal' and 'If I could live my life over, I would change almost nothing'.[2] And the General Health Questionnaire (GHQ)[3] covers a range of negative thoughts and feelings about worry, sleep loss, ability to concentrate and so on. Self-descriptions in those terms call for reflection and mental processing – attending to and remembering particular elements and episodes, interpreting, evaluating and integrating what is recalled and perhaps making comparisons with other people or other situations.

A domain-specific form of happiness that has received considerable research attention is satisfaction with one's job. Questionnaires have asked about satisfaction alone (e.g., 'all things considered, how satisfied are you with your job') or – more often – brought together several different reactions into an overall scale score. For example, widely used multi-item scales labelled as job satisfaction include statements like 'Most days I am enthusiastic about my work' and 'I find real enjoyment in my work'[4] or request ratings of, for instance, 'worthwhile' and 'ideal'.[5]

These compound scales can often extend beyond the true meaning of satisfaction itself. That term derives from the Latin *satis*, indicating 'enough', so the term signals a relatively passive acceptance that something is adequate – 'satisfactory' rather than 'outstanding'. Being 'satisfied with' something is a low-activation response (see below), and for greater accuracy, it should be studied in low-activation terms rather than through enthusiasm, enjoyment, involvement, feelings of worth and so on. We should always look beyond a scale title to check that it is matched by its items.

HEDONIC MEASURES (2): FEELINGS

The second type of hedonic wellbeing measure focuses on happiness feelings, sometimes described by psychologists as 'core affects' – 'primitive, universal, and simple, irreducible on the mental plane'.[6] Affects range along a good-to-bad continuum of 'valence' and occur throughout waking life within emotions, moods,[7] values, attitudes, orientations, prejudices and ideologies. All those involve happiness at some level of scope – feature-specific, domain-specific or global.

In studying hedonic wellbeing through measures of affect, an established perspective is in terms of the circumplex shown below in Figure 2.1.[8] This treats feelings not only in terms of valence but also

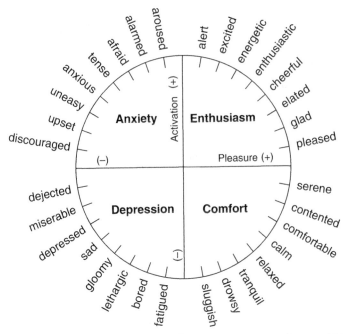

Figure 2.1 Affective wellbeing in terms of positive or negative valence and high or low activation. The quadrant labels Anxiety and Depression refer here only to negative feelings and not to clinical conditions. (*Author's version of the established affective circumplex.*)

through low-to-high mental arousal or activation – a person's 'state of readiness for action or energy expenditure'.[9]

Experiences in terms of those two axes are illustrated around the outside of Figure 2.1, and summary labels for each quadrant's content are indicated as Anxiety (activated negative affect), Enthusiasm (activated positive affect), Depression (low-activation negative affect) and Comfort (low-activation positive affect).[10] Particular feelings of happiness and unhappiness can be represented by their location in the circumplex – their nature in terms of valence and activation and their intensity through distance from the midpoint. Experiences toward the outside of the diagram are more intense. You might like to consider where your feelings have typically been located today.

Figure 2.1 is important for discussions throughout this book. Experiences of hedonic happiness and unhappiness are not restricted to feeling good or feeling bad (affective 'valence'); they also differ in their activation. For example, positive feelings may be either joyful pleasure (activated feelings at the top-right of Figure 2.1) or contented peace of mind (at the bottom-right).

What about the circumplex location of compound measures of happiness, discussed in the previous section? Research has rarely considered those in terms of valence and activation. However, studies in job settings have drawn attention to conceptual overlaps between the affect quadrant here labelled as Enthusiasm and compound scales of work engagement, between the Comfort quadrant and scales of job satisfaction, between Depression and job burnout and (perhaps) Anxiety with workaholism.[11] There is clearly scope to extend valence-and-activation thinking to other compound forms of happiness and unhappiness.

CHAPTER 2: SOME TAKE-HOME MESSAGES

Happiness and unhappiness have often been discussed through labels ('enthusiasm', 'interest', 'distress', 'strain' and so on), which seem to hide their relevance to this book. The constructs are everywhere, even though they may not be described as happiness or unhappiness. Hedonic forms have been investigated in two parallel ways: (a) through multi-item questionnaires that tap compounds of different thoughts and feelings, for example, in terms of life satisfaction, happiness or strain; and (b) through self-reports of experienced feelings, for example, within the affective circumplex. In all cases, it is necessary to consider both valence and activation.

3

FLOURISHING WELLBEING
Self-worth and a good life

Until recently, psychological research into happiness focussed almost exclusively on hedonic concepts and measures, as outlined in Chapter 2. Much less attention has been paid to wellbeing in terms of flourishing. As we'll see, different investigators have different ideas about the nature of that, and they've measured it in a variety of ways. Their different definitions and measures have made it difficult to combine perspectives into one overall framework.

The construct of flourishing wellbeing draws from writings about eudaimonia by Aristotle (384–322 BC) and other ancient Greek philosophers, although their notions have been substantially modified by recent psychologists. The word *eudaimonia* brings together Greek *eu* (good) and *daimon* (spirit) in the idea that we each have our own *daimon* to contribute to achieving our full potential. Within philosophical attempts to characterize a good life (in contrast to one defined merely in terms of hedonic pleasure), eudaimonia is thought to come from personal fulfilment through virtuous behaviour and the pursuit of goals that are intrinsically worthwhile.

Psychologists' models of 'flourishing', the term widely used in preference to 'eudaimonia', often bring in themes of personal fulfilment, but additional aspects have also been introduced. Huta and Waterman (2014) have identified the primary approaches adopted by

11 principal researchers in this field, finding that two broad categories are present in all the perspectives they review. Bringing together aspects of flourishing with very similar meanings, the two general categories were labelled as '*growth/self-realization/self-actualization/development of potentials/full functioning/maturity*' and as '*meaning/purpose/long-term perspective/caring about and contributing to the broader context*'. Huta and Waterman (2014) identified two additional theme-sets in nine of the 11 frameworks and yet another two in three cases. Their analysis indicates that all theorists consider self-realization and a personal sense of meaning to be central to flourishing wellbeing, but in addition each theory emphasises its own themes.

The first general set ('*growth/self-realization/self/actualization/development of potentials/full functioning/maturity*') can be illustrated by the work of Alan Waterman, an early proponent of more-than-hedonism. His 1993 paper[1] emphasized self-realization through 'personal expressiveness' – active striving for excellence and the fulfilment of personally significant potentials, as in the development of one's skills and talents. For Carol Ryff, personal growth is the aspect of positive functioning that 'comes closest to Aristotle's notion of eudaimonia'.[2] She viewed the growth of one's potential, a sense of meaning and continued development as central to 'psychological wellbeing',[3] measuring that through items in six self-descriptive scales – purpose in life, personal growth, autonomy, environmental mastery, positive relationships with others and self-acceptance.[4] Martin Seligman has also emphasized that flourishing wellbeing includes striving for valued outcomes, especially by identifying and developing one's unique strengths, for example, in the service of other people.[5]

Other theorists stressing the importance of personal growth include Richard Ryan and Edward Deci. Their eudaimonic framework is built around the notion that happiness derives from satisfaction of three basic needs – for autonomy, competence and relatedness. Flourishing is said to come through the attainment of 'intrinsic' goals in those areas – ones that are self-chosen, personally attractive and optimally challenging.[6]

This first aspect of flourishing wellbeing thus concerns a sense of personal development through progress towards goals that are somehow worthwhile[7] and move one towards personal improvement. The notion that each of us might somehow be 'more than we are now' or perhaps 'better than we are now' can be hard to grasp and might be illustrated through its partial similarity with physical recovery after an illness or injury. Our sick body gradually recovers to attain good health – as if some notion of our true physical state is available as a goal and we develop towards that state. And of course each person's physical health can be influenced by lifestyle and specific actions. So it is with a 'psychologically better me' – like a 'physically better me'; that goal state exists and can be influenced, although we can't always identify it.

The second broad category in every flourishing perspective reviewed by Huta and Waterman ('meaning/purpose/long-term perspective/caring about and contributing to the broader context') includes concepts in the model developed by Brian Little.[8] This model explores the meaningfulness of personal projects to an individual in terms of consistency with values, commitments and other aspects of self-identity.

Carol Ryff has a more long-term perspective on flourishing across one's life as a whole, emphasizing that a sense of purpose in life is essential. Also writing about life in general, Martin Seligman argues that 'the meaningful life consists in belonging to and serving something you believe is bigger than the self'.[9] Several inputs from the environment have been shown to be differently associated with life's perceived meaningfulness versus hedonic happiness. For instance, personal stressors are strongly linked to poor hedonic wellbeing but uncorrelated with meaningfulness, and positive social contributions are more correlated with meaningfulness than with hedonic wellbeing.[10]

As a final example of flourishing themes, let's consider Huta and Waterman's category 'engagement/interest/flow', which is present in four of the 11 models they considered. For example, central to Seligman's conception of flourishing is absorption in issues beyond oneself. Short-term experiences of engagement have been explored in terms of 'flow', becoming psychologically immersed in a challenging activity,[11] and more extended engagement is sometimes viewed as 'thriving', perhaps including a desire for new learning and personal development.[12] Linked to these more recent perspectives, effort-expenditure has long been viewed as an aspect of happiness despite current strain, if that effort is directed at outcomes that are personally valued.[13]

In overview, there is widespread agreement that the principal forms of flourishing emphasize self-realization and the experience of meaning and purpose, but additional themes have been included by different theorists, and those researchers often diverge from each other by concentrating on certain elements rather than others.

HOW MIGHT WE MEASURE FLOURISHING WELLBEING?

It's clear from this summary that the concept of flourishing is more diffuse and difficult to define than is hedonic wellbeing. Measurement has been through self-report questionnaires, often with items referring only to a researcher's own model of flourishing or to a part of the overall construct. These can sometimes be criticized in respect of content validity (are they truly addressing the concept of flourishing?) and for a lack of evidence about links with relevant variables (the scale's 'concurrent' or 'predictive' validity). Against that background, let's look at some questionnaire items that can illustrate how psychologists have interpreted the notion of flourishing.

The Questionnaire for Eudaimonic Wellbeing devised by Alan Waterman and colleagues[14] covers a range of elements through 21 self-report items such as 'It is important for me to feel fulfilled by the activities that I engage in', 'I feel best when I'm doing something worth investing a great deal of effort in', 'My life is centred around a set of core beliefs that give meaning to my life' and 'I believe I have discovered who I really am'.[15] The source publication reports validity evidence from two samples of university students in the United States through predicted associations with other variables; subsequent validity studies in South Africa and India have also been restricted to student samples.[16]

The Flourishing Scale by Ed Diener and colleagues[17] covers a more limited set of themes but in addition asks about social relationships and personal optimism. Eight items include 'I lead a purposeful and meaningful life', 'I am engaged and interested in my daily activities' and 'My social relationships are supportive and rewarding'.[18] The source paper brings together findings from six samples of US university students and reports significant associations with other relevant scales. Additional validity evidence has been reported from India and New Zealand.[19]

Focussing on a single element within flourishing, the Meaning in Life questionnaire examines 'what makes your life feel important to you'. This contains ten items, five of which ask about the perceived presence of meaning and five of which record a person's search for meaning. The 'presence' set includes 'I understand my life's meaning' and 'I have a good sense of what makes my life meaningful'.[20] Focussing on a job domain, the Work and Meaning Inventory examines the perceived meaningfulness of paid work. The ten items include 'I understand how my work contributes to my life's meaning' and 'I view my work as contributing to my personal growth'.[21]

Flourishing wellbeing has sometimes been studied in terms of 'thriving'. The Comprehensive Inventory of Thriving contains 54 self-report items, from which ten items are drawn for the Brief Inventory of Thriving.[22] Those include 'I am achieving most of my goals', 'I feel a sense of belonging in my community' and 'My life is going well'.[23] Asking specifically about activities in paid work, another thriving scale[24] contains two five-item subscales to obtain self-reports about personal development (labelled as 'learning') and a sense of vitality. The learning subscale contains items like 'I see myself continually improving' and 'I am developing a lot as a person', and vitality is covered by items such as 'I feel alert and awake' and 'I am looking forward to each new day'.

Subjective vitality itself has been measured in context-free terms through a scale containing seven items similar to those in the scale immediately above, such as 'I feel alive and vital' and 'I look forward to each new day'. Positive correlations with measures of self-actualization and self-esteem are substantial, as are negative correlations with anxiety, depression and other indicators of poor mental health.[25]

It's clear that flourishing wellbeing has been operationalized in a variety of ways and that these overlap only partially. Researchers have different conceptual starting points and use different measures, so the potential for agreement about a single perspective is limited. Some of the items are very abstract and can be difficult to understand, and the construct is in danger of becoming excessively broad as more and more elements are introduced. For instance, personal resilience (the capacity to maintain wellbeing in the face of adversity) is emphasized in more recent discussions but is absent from earlier models.

FITTING TOGETHER HEDONIC AND FLOURISHING WELLBEING

For many people, some flourishing themes can seem unconnected to their daily life. If you are struggling to obtain an adequate income or otherwise to cope with prolonged adversity, fulfilling personally significant potentials or becoming absorbed in issues beyond oneself can seem laughably irrelevant. Carol Ryff recognized that her perspective 'may be faulted for creating yardsticks of self-evaluation that are unattainable, unattractive, or irrelevant for individuals at different locations in the social structure'; she pointed out that notions of flourishing 'are essentially manifestations of middle-class values'.[26]

In addition to potential nonapplicability, flourishing research has suffered from the vagueness or ambiguity of some of its terms. Questionnaire items like 'I believe I have discovered who I really am' or 'I understand my life's meaning' are open to multiple interpretations or don't really make sense to some people. Flourishing concepts are inherently complex and difficult to understand, but user-friendly clarification is essential for moving the field forward.

Finally, it's important to consider possible causal patterns that link together hedonic and flourishing wellbeing. A framework of separate operation seems to have been generally assumed in this field.

However, studies with a range of measures have pointed to substantial statistical overlap between wellbeing of the two kinds, and several researchers have emphasized that hedonic and flourishing happiness may not be separable in practice.[27] Perhaps the two kinds together 'reflect one overarching wellbeing construct'.[28]

That appears to be the view taken by researcher Martin Seligman, who has argued that the elements within flourishing are among the several kinds of building blocks that make up wellbeing.[29] Just as happiness has traditionally been examined through life satisfaction and different forms of affect, it can also be studied as experienced meaning, sense of purpose or social engagement; in that way, it can be viewed as comprising a range of experiences which vary in their emphasis on hedonic versus flourishing content. Rather than being separate forms of wellbeing, the two kinds of happiness intermingle in a variety of overlapping ways.

CHAPTER 3: SOME TAKE-HOME MESSAGES

In addition to the conventionally studied hedonic wellbeing, flourishing is essential to happiness in its fullest sense. However, the notion is difficult to define and study. It involves experiences of personal fulfilment and experienced meaning, beyond which an agreed conceptual or operational definition has yet to be found. In addition, questionnaires to measure flourishing wellbeing and its separate components have often been less than ideal, with items that are difficult to understand and possibly irrelevant to many individuals. Rather than being two separate and parallel kinds of wellbeing, the forms of each might be considered as interrelated building blocks of the more general construct of happiness.

4

INFLUENCES FROM THE
WORLD AROUND YOU
Nine principal features

It's obvious that events in your world and the conditions that surround you have a major impact on your happiness or unhappiness, and psychologists have carried out a large number of investigations to explore key environmental influences of that kind. This chapter will develop some themes from those studies.

First, we should look again at the three levels of scope introduced in Chapter 1. *Feature-specific* happiness or unhappiness is restricted to feelings about one particular thing, person, idea or activity, for instance, satisfaction with your apartment or house. This narrowest form is central to experiences of all kinds and in all reactions to your surroundings. *Domain-specific* happiness or unhappiness is concerned with a particular segment of life, for example, feelings about your family life, your job or your health. *Context-free* happiness or unhappiness, with the broadest scope, covers life in general – your global wellbeing, life satisfaction and so on. Features affecting this global level are also important for more narrow-scope happiness, but additional features loom large in particular settings. For example, job satisfaction is much affected by your boss and colleagues. The present chapter will first consider aspects of your world that affect *context-free* wellbeing and then look briefly at some particular domains.

Any identification of principal sources must decide how many categories are appropriate, and reaching that decision requires us to balance precise specification against practical feasibility. Small numbers of categories (for instance, merely demands or supports in the environment) are likely to yield undesirably broad groupings; for instance, the large category of 'demands' contains many different features, and those operate in their own different ways. And although a larger number of categories can allow more detailed precision, the number can easily become too many to handle. A compromise is needed, and different wellbeing researchers have suggested alternative but overlapping lists of primary sources. The compromise made here draws on thousands of research studies to identify nine environmental features that have been found to affect happiness and unhappiness. They can be described as:

1 Personal influence – being able to affect what happens
2 Using your abilities – applying your skills
3 Demands and goals – what you have to do
4 Variety – different activities
5 Clear requirements and outlook – not too much uncertainty
6 Contacts with other people – enough and good dealings with others
7 Money – at least enough to live on
8 Adequate physical setting – housing, equipment, etc.
9 A valued role – doing something felt to be worthwhile

The first – and essential – aspect of any setting is the possibility of some *personal influence*. In order to gain something positive or to get out of harm's way, you must be able to control some of the things you want to happen. You don't necessarily want influence in a big way – running a large company or being a government minister – but you mustn't feel powerless and completely at the mercy of events.

This is important for you to avoid pain and maybe achieve some pleasure, but also because it creates a sense of your free existence or 'agency' – not just something pushed around by whatever happens.

German psychologists around 1900 recognized children's 'joy in being a cause', and American researchers in the 1950s emphasized being an 'origin' rather than a 'pawn'.

Many research investigations have found significant associations between the level of a person's opportunity for personal influence and his or her wellbeing. In part, this connection arises because influence over events means you can change other features to make them better for you and – conceivably – for others around you. On the other hand, if you're completely lacking in feature number one with no personal influence over your life, you can't get into settings where, for instance, you can use your abilities (feature number two) or be exposed to more variety (number four). And of course, your level of personal influence is itself affected by some of the other features. For instance, a lack of money (number seven) means that you can less change things to make you happier.

The second feature essential for happiness is *using your abilities*. People need the possibility of applying their skills, doing what they're good at, both in order to solve problems and achieve goals and also because it's often satisfying in its own right to employ skill and expertise. People take satisfaction from doing well; they like to feel competent.

Everyone has over the years acquired a huge range of skilled behaviours. These may involve quite simple routines that have become so automatic that we don't realize how expert we are. In other cases, we recognize that we're applying personal knowledge to solve problems in a way that many other people could not do. Generally, the opportunity to be effective in skilful activities is important for feeling good about yourself and the maintenance of self-confidence; in job settings, workers see this as part of fulfilling their potential – a key aspect of flourishing wellbeing described in the last chapter.

Third among the nine happiness-influencing features are some *demands and goals* from the environment – being required to do something. Although happiness often depends on achieving goals that you've set yourself, it also comes from targets introduced through a role. Because you're a carer for your family, an employee in a certain job, a member of a sports club, a local councillor or in almost any other role, you become required to aim for certain goals. And those externally-set goals force you to take action, strive in ways you otherwise wouldn't, experience some obstacles and maybe make you happy because in the end you achieve something you value.

Habitual activities in a role can themselves be pleasant, as people experience the comfort of repetition, although (as we'll consider later) you can certainly have 'too much of a good thing'. The general point is that external demands bring more than unhappiness; they may sometimes be unwelcome, but in many cases people come to find in them something they value. Happiness benefits can also derive from other features linked to demands, such as being required to use your abilities (number two) or having to interact with other people (number six).

Responding to external demands through getting things done can contribute to feelings of self-esteem, in part through the achievement of intermediate goals. Many complex projects extend over weeks or months and require a series of interim successes at different times. These intervening achievements provide their own inputs to happiness in addition to the pleasure of overall success. Furthermore, people are often working through several projects at once, each with its interim successes or failures, and overall happiness or unhappiness frequently comes through the mixture of feelings arising from those different activities.

The fourth main happiness-affecting feature is some *variety* in your life. Being stuck in one place or doing the same thing over and over again gets people down. That's partly because of processes of adaptation to an unchanging input – we get 'used to' things (see the next chapter) and can't enjoy happiness-inducing contrasts between stimuli – but also because low-variety settings often lack other happiness-promoting features: ability use, social contact and so on. For those kinds of reason, variety is often called 'the spice of life'.

The fifth desirable aspect of any setting is its potential for understanding what may happen to you. Research has repeatedly shown that having *clear requirements and outlook* is important for happiness in many situations, whereas not knowing what to do and being unable to predict the outcome of your actions can cause a lot of anxiety. This requirement arises partly from the practical issue that it's essential to be able to envisage possible outcomes when deciding what to do next; decisions and plans have to be based on some kind of prediction. Low levels of clarity about your situation and what the future holds can be very disturbing, such that people after a long period of uncertainty can feel the need to 'do something, even anything' to bring it to an end.

Sixth are *contacts with other people*. These are clearly important in lots of ways, and their absence is often a source of depression. Social interactions are essential for us to feel less lonely and develop friendships, and other people can help to solve problems as well as provide comfort when we are upset – providing both 'instrumental' and 'emotional' support. It can be refreshing to chat with acquaintances, even those you don't particularly like. In addition, many goals can only be achieved by working with others, both because more contributors become available and because other people may have different skills and concerns.

Social contacts are also important to help you to understand yourself better, through processes of social comparison. Everyone needs to compare opinions and abilities against those of other people in order to evaluate and understand oneself based on a wider set of views. And it's from other people that you learn what behaviours and thoughts are appropriate in your network; social norms and local fashions can affect ideas and opinions as much as they influence clothes and musical preferences.

The general category of social contacts should be viewed in terms of both their number and their quality. In respect of number, a complete absence of other people (as when living alone entirely at home or in solitary confinement) is upsetting and can distort understanding of oneself and other people. We need to have some contact with other people for emotional and practical benefits.

In respect of quality, social contacts can of course be negative as well as positive. 'Agony aunts' writing in popular magazines devote much of their space to difficulties in intimate relationships, and dealing with a partner, friends or colleagues can sometimes be difficult, boring or actively unpleasant. Research has emphasized many negative consequences from being bullied at work or at school, often focussing on 'cyberbullying' through social media or other internet systems. The general point here is that both quantity and quality of social contact have been shown repeatedly to influence a person's happiness or unhappiness; social contacts can be negative as well as positive.

Interactions with other people are often within a social role, and established routines within that role can provide many of the other desirable inputs in this chapter. For example, membership of a religious group can have spiritual benefits, but it also brings about contact with other people and introduces activities and goals that structure one's time. Hedonic wellbeing is typically found to be slightly higher among members of formal religious groups,[1] as are aspects of flourishing such as personal growth and experienced purpose in life.[2]

An important feature whose absence creates unhappiness is of course *money* (number seven). When your own and your family's requirements continually exceed the money that you have, it's clear that you may struggle to keep going and to escape despair. As well as problems in paying for food and other essential items, a lack of money means you can't do much to improve other beneficial features described here, like variety (number four) or social interactions (six) which need money – for the pub, club, cinema or similar. And poverty can be self-perpetuating, as poor people often have to pay more for what they buy, can't afford money-saving equipment, can only pay one bill by leaving others unpaid and may be stuck with high interest charges on loans taken out to meet emergencies. People with low incomes also have to spend a higher proportion of their money on food, leaving proportionately less to buy things for enjoyment or fun. Linked to issues of that kind, research has frequently shown that on average distress and unhappiness are worst among poorer individuals.[3]

The eighth feature essential for happiness is an *adequate physical setting* – your living conditions, home, furniture, heating, neighbourhood and so on. Everyone needs to be protected against physical threat and to have reasonable heating, space and facilities for everyday living. Some physical settings are very inadequate in these respects, and naturally they wear down any potential feelings of happiness. In addition to its own direct impact, a poor physical setting often occurs in combination with other environmental problems in the list, such as a lack of money or personal influence, and those collectively work to depress wellbeing.

Finally it's important for happiness that you are doing something you can believe in, at least from time to time. A *valued role* (feature number nine) provides some benefits for other people as well as merely for yourself – as a parent, a worker, a member of a community association or whatever. For example, recent increases in the average age of many countries' population have increased the need for carers to assist older people living at home. Those carers usually receive only low wages, but as one said, 'It's all about knowing I can help. I'm doing something that matters to people, and I'll work hard at that'. People in unpleasant jobs (cleaners of public toilets, animal exterminators and the like) often emphasize the ways in which their activities are socially valuable, and people who are self-employed rank their place in society significantly above the self-ranking of those who are employed.[4]

Having a valued role is thus partly a question of how you see yourself: are some of your activities personally fulfilling, the kind of thing you think it's worth spending your time on? But in addition to your own perception, this ninth feature also covers esteem or recognition from others: how is your role valued in society or in that part of society that matters to you?

In summary, the importance of these nine environmental sources of happiness has been confirmed by many research investigations, and we can be confident about their major impact on subjective wellbeing. They are individually important, but they can operate together as a group of positive or negative influences. For example, people who lack money are likely to be short of other features in the list, whereas more wealthy people are freed from many of the restraints.

The general importance of these nine aspects of the world applies to all parts of life. Each of your settings (for instance, your social world or your job) can be described in the same nine terms: they affect your happiness in similar ways wherever you are. However, for domain-specific happiness, it's usually necessary to supplement the general account with additional issues. For instance, high or low family-related wellbeing is likely to derive substantially from the nature of the emotional relationship between partners and (where appropriate) the characteristics and behaviour of children. For family-related well-being, those two must be added to the nine always-important features covered here. Similarly, wellbeing in a job depends on having a supportive boss, possessing reasonable career prospects, and being treated fairly, as well as the nine universally important features considered above.[5] In accounting for sources of wellbeing in the environment, the current list of nine features is always crucial, but we also need to look at additional themes that are specific to the domain in question.

TOO MUCH OF A GOOD THING?

Research has almost never asked about the shape of environmental features' impact: is an increment in one of the features accompanied by an increment in wellbeing to the same degree no matter how much of that feature is already present? In other words, is the relationship a straight line ('linear') one, or is it curved in some way ('non-linear')? Extremely high feature levels can create overload. If you're organizing a family, struggling with problems in your job, looking after your elderly parents and trying to juggle events in a social life, you're not likely to want more demands and goals (feature number three). You'd like fewer rather than more.

We should thus ask whether people want more and more of the key happiness features without a limit or whether they are increasingly desirable only up to a moderate level. Perhaps the beneficial features reach a tipping point, after which further increases in their amount (for instance, having still more goals to meet) actually reduce your wellbeing.

That up-and-down pattern has been documented for several of the nine features, although very few studies have explored the possibility.[6] As in the example above, it's been established for number three (demands and goals) that you want some requirements (avoiding 'underload') but not too much pressure (avoiding 'overload'). And it's also important for the first feature (having some influence over events). Although a moderate personal impact on things is essential for your self-esteem and feelings of wellbeing, if your environment (in a job, at home or wherever) forces you to make too many controlling decisions, you become anxious, worried about making mistakes, overburdened with problems to solve and generally not happy.

Very high levels of variety (number four) are also of this kind. You can end up with so many different decisions to make that you can't really concentrate properly on any of them, you can't find time to develop expertise in particular areas (feature two), and the different kinds of required activities get in each other's way. That pattern has also been found for inputs from other people (feature number six). Excessive levels of interpersonal contact can harm wellbeing through overcrowding, lack of privacy, reduced personal control and frequent interruptions to goal-directed activity. All over the world, societies have established guidelines and physical structures to prevent the disruption of happiness through overly high social interaction

In the cases illustrated so far, the happiness pattern is nonlinear in the form of an upside-down U. Starting at a very low level of a feature, as you get more opportunity for (say) influencing your activities, you gradually become more positive, moving up the left-hand side of an inverted U. Then with still more personal control, your happiness starts to level off before you slip down the other side of the upside-down U as the requirements become more than you can handle.

Happiness-promoting features with the inverted-U are the first six in the list considered here: personal influence, using your abilities, demands and goals, variety, clear requirements and outlook and contacts with other people. Although greater amounts of these make you happier up to medium-high levels, very large amounts are on average likely to become harmful – too much of a good thing.

However, the final three of the nine features work in a slightly different way. From a low starting point, increases in numbers seven to nine (money, adequate physical setting and a valued role) are likely to bring more happiness, but after a medium-high amount, they make on average no difference. At high to very high levels, as people get more and more of those three features, they are on average similarly happy with no general decrease or increase in their wellbeing.

For example, the amount people earn (feature number seven) is apparently not related on average to their happiness in the inverted-U way expected for features one to six. Money certainly matters a lot when you haven't got much, so increasing your income from a very low level definitely increases happiness on average. But research has shown that happiness stops going up with continuing increases in income beyond moderately high levels without on average then going down. Several studies have shown a strong association between income and happiness for poorer people, but further increases after a moderate level of income have only a limited impact on happiness, and an average levelling-off rather than a general reduction is found.[7]

Of course, people and their situations vary. Some lottery winners do become unhappy with their sudden riches, although on average differences between very high levels of wealth do not affect wellbeing. Money no longer matters on a day-to-day basis when you're wealthy; other aspects of life become more important to you. So for feature number seven, the nonlinear pattern is one of a strong association between income and happiness only across low to medium-high levels of income. More money certainly makes you happier when you're poor, but increased amounts don't matter much when you're very rich; the average difference in happiness between having a very large income and an even larger one is negligible.

The list of environmental contributors thus contains two kinds of happiness-promoting feature – some for which extremely large amounts become harmful (identified above as the first six features in the list) and others (features seven to nine) where increasingly high levels continue to make people happy but where the actual high level of the feature doesn't much matter – illustrated by differences in very large amounts of money.

The two patterns are similar to differences between the impacts of two kinds of vitamin on physical health. Vitamins are essential for health but only up to a point; after a certain level of intake is reached, increased doses don't help and may even harm you. With that in mind, 'guideline daily amounts' or 'recommended daily allowances' have been published for many vitamins.

It's rather like that for happiness: without the nine features, you're unhappy (just as a lack of vitamins impairs health), but when your intake has reached a moderate level (like the recommended daily allowance), consuming more won't help and may indeed harm you. The present approach has in those respects been described as a 'Vitamin Model', and the two sets of features have been seen to yield either an 'additional decrement' (AD, the first six) or a 'constant effect' (CE, numbers seven to nine).[8]

The average AD and CE happiness patterns are shown in Figure 4.1. A single curve describes the pattern at lower levels of a feature, and after a midrange plateau two curves diverge at higher levels.

PROFILES OF HAPPINESS POTENTIAL

In these ways, any setting or domain can be described in terms of the nine features, so we can suggest every situation's happiness potential in the nine respects. Where does your domestic situation fall on each dimension? Or your job, your social life, your neighbourhood or particular activities? We can also create the same nine-feature profile for situations that you imagine, comparing in those terms your current setting against a possible alternative job, social group or whatever. And we can work out possible changes in each of those respects, using the nine features to make your life better. Many practical benefits can flow from what started as an academic exercise.

In this short overview, let's take a brief look at how profiles of happiness potential might be explored in some life settings – in unemployment, retirement, homemaking and several kinds of jobs.

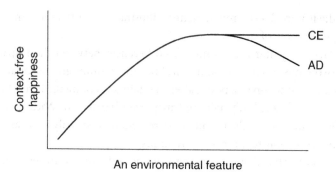

An environmental feature

Figure 4.1 You can have too much of a good thing (AD, an 'additional decrement') for some aspects of your world, but for others a still greater increase doesn't on average make much difference after a moderate level (CE, a 'constant effect').

Unemployment

Most people spend large parts of their life in a paid job, but at certain times a minority are forced into unemployment. How does that change the nine happiness features? It's no surprise that on average unemployed people suffer in each respect. Personal influence (feature one) is low, as unemployed people have less chance to decide and act as they wish. And lack of success in job-seeking and increased dependence on welfare bureaucracies all reduce control of what happens. That low level of personal influence is harmful both in its own right (feeling powerless is demoralizing) and also because it brings an inability to affect other key features; unemployed people can't do much to improve their variety, financial position or physical situation.

Opportunities for using your abilities (feature number two) are also typically reduced during unemployment; people can no longer apply skills in a job, and for many there is little chance to gain new ones. Third, demands and goals also decline, as time schedules and job pressures are removed, and the environment less promotes purposeful activity. Several investigators have confirmed that unemployed people can have difficulty filling their days, with long periods spent without activity, merely sitting around or watching television.

A decline during unemployment in the fourth happiness feature, variety, occurs in part because of the reduction in goals and demands (feature three) and also from a loss of welcome contrast between job and nonjob activities; everything can seem the same. The fifth happiness feature (clear requirements and outlook) is also harmed, as life becomes less predictable, outcomes of job-seeking are uncertain, and you lack future information which is essential for decisions about your family and yourself.

Relationships with other people (feature number six) can also take a beating during unemployment; social involvement can be reduced by a low income, and family harmony can be destroyed by disputes about limited financial resources. Reduced money (feature seven) is almost always a problem, as low income can block the purchase of basic necessities. In addition, a linked shift to financial dependence on other family members can often strain relationships even more. Low levels of the eighth characteristic (adequate physical setting) are usually associated during unemployment with low availability of money; the living conditions of unemployed individuals can be really bad, for instance, because they can't pay for heating repairs or replacing everyday items.

Finally, a valued role (feature nine) is clearly lost by enforced joblessness. On becoming unemployed, a person is moved out of a socially approved position and the positive self-evaluations that go with it. You're no longer a breadwinner, and you may not feel a full member of society. Even when welfare benefits remove the worst financial hardship, there may be shame attached to receiving public funds and a seeming failure to provide for one's family or to contribute to society more widely.

In a nutshell, research has confirmed that on average unemployed people are substantially more unhappy than workers in a job, and has pointed to the impact of the nine features in this chapter. But of course some unemployed individuals are even less happy than others are. That's largely because different unemployed environments provide different amounts of the nine features, but also because a social setting and local norms are important − feelings can be influenced by what happens to other people. Is your lack of a job different from everyone around you, or is unemployment quite usual in your community? Several investigations have found that unwanted joblessness is less painful when it's more common. For example, economist Andrew Clark showed that the impact of unemployment on wellbeing depended on the reference level in one's region or household – 'loosely speaking, unemployment hurts less the more of it there is around'.[9]

In addition to the moderating influence of a local community, unhappiness during unemployment can also be influenced by people's attitudes, needs and other characteristics. An obvious difference is in terms of age, and it's medium-aged individuals who have been found to suffer the most in unemployment; they're often the ones who need to provide for a family and meet its considerable requirement for money.

It's also essential to consider differences between people's motivation. Some unemployed people want to have a job more strongly than others, and the ones who particularly desire a job (described formally as having greater 'employment commitment') are consistently found to be the most distressed in their situation. Linked to that, many people who adapt to unemployment by gradually reducing their commitment to paid work come to experience less distress – their lack of a job no longer matters so much to them, perhaps because they have found other ways to build into their lives some of the nine happiness features described here.

Retirement, homemaking and jobs

We've seen for unemployment that, in addition to general patterns of influence ('main effects' in statistical analyses), aspects of the person are also important, perhaps as 'moderators' of those effects. That's the theme throughout this chapter: happiness or unhappiness can be interpreted largely in terms of the nine features, but aspects of a person are likely also to be involved. Personal contributors to wellbeing will be reviewed in the next chapter, but let's first take a brief look at three other life settings.

Retirement

Studies that compare matched groups of retired and still-working people have found that happiness is overall roughly the same for the two groups; on average, retirement doesn't affect happiness or unhappiness one way or the other. But there are wide differences around the average. Some people who retire from paid work prefer their new life, whereas others feel their life has been emptied of much that is desirable.

As you might expect by now, these individual differences are largely a question of the nine happiness features. Some retired people have adequate money, stimulating activities and positive social relationships, whereas the life of others is lacking in many of the key features. Research has shown that retired people whose world contains high levels of most of them are substantially happier than those retired people who experience low levels. For example, some retired people have moderate levels of goals and demands. They benefit from satisfying routines and targets[10] (within feature three) and gain satisfaction from interesting tasks well done; many benefits of paid work can be replicated without a job.

Homemaking

What about women, or increasingly men, who stay at home rather than having a paid job? As with retirement, research has made it clear that on average those two groups are equally happy, but again there are wide individual differences. Published studies have almost always focussed on women, and as usual we need to consider the nine aspects of happiness potential and differences between people. Some stay-at-home individuals have desirably high levels of the nine features – they are using their abilities and have adequate money, good social contacts, a varied schedule and so on. Others may be restricted to simple, repeated childcare, be short of money and social stimulation and generally score lower on the features of this chapter. Unsurprisingly, members of the second group are likely to have worse wellbeing, although we need to be on the lookout for people who are beyond the tipping point for imposed demands and other features.

However, person-based moderating variables also matter, for example, individual differences in role preference. Some people are happy that raising their family is a rewarding full-time job, and they need few other happiness features in their life, whereas others are unhappy with the restrictions of domestic life. As in other cases, well-being depends partly on which role you want.[11]

Jobs

Psychologists have studied each of the nine features in paid work from a variety of perspectives and often in great detail, and the book's Vitamin Model was originally developed with jobs in mind. As is necessary for happiness-profiles in all kinds of setting, some features must be added for domain-specific application. In respect of job settings, we need additionally to focus on a supportive boss, reasonable career prospects and being treated fairly. Unsurprisingly, worker happiness and unhappiness have regularly been found to depend on the nine general and the three domain-specific features cited here.[12]

In sum, the nine features in this chapter have a general importance, so that any life chunk (for instance, your family life, your social world, your job or your staying at home) can be described in the same nine terms: they affect happiness in similar ways wherever you are.

CHAPTER 4: SOME TAKE-HOME MESSAGES

Happiness in any role depends on experiencing enough of nine main features – personal influence, ability use, moderate demands and goals, variety, clear requirements and outlook, contacts with other people, money, adequate physical setting and a valued role. However, associations between these features and happiness are unlikely to take the form of a straight line. Instead desirable levels are always in the medium-to-high range, and in many cases extremely high levels bring about a happiness decrement. For summarizing the happiness potential of any setting – actual or possible – it can be helpful to think in terms of a nine-feature profile, reviewing how a position stands in each of the nine respects. In addition, for domain-specific happiness, a small number of features specific to each domain need to be added to the always-important nine.

5

INFLUENCES FROM WITHIN YOURSELF

In the last chapter, we looked at how nine important aspects of the world make us happy or unhappy. Yet feelings don't just come from the environment; they also come from ourselves. As the English poet William Cowper wrote in 1782,

> Happiness depends, as Nature shows,
> Less on exterior things than most suppose.

In many cases, subjective wellbeing isn't simply a response to an external event, like an electric light that has been switched on. Instead our feelings can be affected by the kind of person we are and the way we interpret something – more like an electric light that can be somewhat different from other electric lights and can be adjusted to make it brighter or dimmer.

Everyone looks at his or her world through filters of memories, comparisons and expectations. Interpretations can be quick and unnoticed in everyday activity or they can be deliberate and based on careful reflection. They influence how Cowper's 'exterior things' are experienced. And, importantly, we all have different memories, comparisons and expectations, so that impacts from a current situation are not always identical for different people. Although the nine 'exterior things' are crucial, their impact can be modified by the perceiver.

This chapter will explore the many ways people can do that. Personal contributions to happiness and unhappiness will be organized in two broad categories – distal sources extended across a period of time and proximal influences that occur in a current situation. In the first case, we'll be concerned with age, gender, personality and similar long-term features, and then we'll turn to processes of appraisal and interpretation.

LONGER-TERM PERSONAL SOURCES OF HAPPINESS

Happiness and inheritance

Let's start with characteristics you are born with – from the genetic lottery of conception. There's no doubt from studies of twins that happiness is partly inherited. Twins from a single fertilized egg ('monozygotic' twins) are genetically almost identical, but dizygotic/nonidentical twins (from two eggs) share about 50 per cent of genes – just like other pairs of siblings. By comparing pairs of each kind of twin reared together against those reared apart (and thus with varied environments), researchers have estimated the relative contribution of genetic and environmental factors. Their studies have indicated that between 35 and 50 per cent of happiness differences are determined by inheritance.[1]

Happiness is not unique in that way. Many other aspects of you derive partly from what you are born with, although genetic impacts are not always simple and immediate. Inheritance often works through person-situation interactions across a number of years. For example, different levels of intelligence and different traits of personality – all substantially inherited – lead people into dissimilar situations (different schools, friendship networks, social settings, work roles and so on), and those different situations have different cumulative effects on feelings and behaviour. Thus higher-intelligence children can differ from others in acquiring qualifications that allow them to move into more complex jobs. And more complex jobs are accompanied by better wellbeing, so that genetic effects on mental ability and personality can indirectly create differences in happiness.

This example points again to the impact of the world around us. Genes don't completely dominate your happiness, which is also influenced by key aspects of the environment as described in Chapter 4. That's the general theme for the present section: long-term personal characteristics can contribute to wellbeing, but each one's influence is partial, and events in your life also make a large difference.

Happiness and age

Turning to individual characteristics, age has often been found to be associated with happiness – in a U-shaped rather than a straight-line pattern. Between the ages of around 20 and the decade between 40 and 50, progressively lower hedonic happiness occurs in comparisons between different age groups, but after the middle period that trend is reversed so that average age-group scores become steadily higher until they level off at about 70.[2] Why might that be? All research has made comparisons between people of different ages rather than following the same individuals across years (difficult to do across several decades), so we should be cautious about suggesting possible trends within individual people.

We need to look for explanations of the happiness U-shape in terms of influences that might change across the years – including of course the nine features in this book. For example, as people move towards middle age, they often take on additional job and family responsibilities, perhaps leading to overload through childcare and commitments to elderly relatives. Conflicts between domestic and other roles can become unusually great in these middle years, and income can increasingly fail to meet expanding needs. So we can see some possible increases in happiness-harming features up to the middle years. But why might happiness on average improve after middle age? In part, it's because negative inputs tend to decline – fewer demands on time and money and reduced uncertainty about the future. As children in the family grow up and as job and other activities become established, life changes for many people mean that, on average, hedonic happiness tends to increase.

Aspects of flourishing wellbeing also differ between groups of different ages. For instance, older individuals report lower personal growth and purpose in life.[3] Other differences can occur because older people tend to see happiness in partly different terms from younger ones. As described in Chapter 1, the two groups emphasize either excitement or peacefulness respectively, and they are likely to adjust their behaviour and associated thoughts to match those preferences.[4] Also important are age differences in how you respond to what happens. For example, we'll look shortly at how people compare themselves against others. In their later years, people are more likely to review how their life has developed, perhaps making more happiness-promoting 'downward' comparisons – recognizing how things might have been worse or how other people are often less happy than they are.

Men and women

On average, men and women report similar levels of life satisfaction, global happiness and job satisfaction,[5] but studies have frequently shown that women are more likely than men to be upset about themselves or their situation. They tend to experience higher levels of worry and anxiety and focus more on troublesome aspects of themselves and their world. We'll see later that women are more likely to engage in harmful rumination, but it's important to note that this male-female difference isn't found for more positive kinds of happiness.

Personality

Happiness levels are also linked to long-term aspects of personality. For example, some people looking at a half-empty glass may view it as almost full whereas others see it as more nearly empty. That general tendency to view the world in positive or negative terms has been assessed by researchers through people's evaluations of a wide range of objects that are considered neutral across a large sample – your telephone number, the climate and so on. A pessimistic general disposition measured in that way has been found to be associated with separately measured feelings of anxiety, depression, low global happiness and low job satisfaction, both at a single time and across later years.[6]

Several traits of personality are linked to this general affective disposition. 'Traits' are identified by examining people's self-descriptions of their typical behaviour and their likes and dislikes in order to find the main groupings that occur together; principal groups of customary behaviours and preferences can be taken to represent a trait of personality. You can find examples of trait-scales by checking 'Scoring Keys' at https://ipip.ori.org/newMultipleconstructs.htm. That website covers traits like adaptability, dutifulness, gregariousness, independence, orderliness, recklessness, sensitivity and timidity.

Personality differences build up over a long time, as associated lifestyles create differential entry to particular situations. For instance, extraverted people tend to move into settings that differ from those entered by less extraverted people, and the consistently varied nature of their activities and associated satisfactions can bring about contrasting levels of happiness. In turn, undertaking and enjoying extraverted activity can strengthen a person's extraversion, so happiness differences linked to personality can become firmly established over a lifetime.

It's currently popular among psychologists to view some personality traits in terms of the 'Big Five' factors. Those are usually named as Neuroticism, Extraversion, Openness to Experience, Agreeableness and Conscientiousness. This way of thinking of people in only five ways is obviously too restricted, but the Big Five do cover a lot of everyone's personality.

Recognizing that most people fall in the middle of each range, *Neuroticism* is usually taken to include high levels of anxiety, depression and moodiness,[7] with low scores sometimes labelled positively as 'emotional stability'. All traits are linked to particular ways of perceiving the world, and high scorers on a Neuroticism scale are more likely to look out for and notice potentially negative features around them. There's also evidence that more Neurotic people tend to move into situations that are potentially harmful. Not surprisingly, conceptual overlap between Neuroticism and unhappiness means that this aspect of continuing personality is strongly associated with more negative feelings in particular situations.[8] Whatever the actual content of a situation, people defined as generally more neurotic in personality terms are likely to be less happy than others.

The second of the Big Five factors, *Extraversion*, involves 'turning outward' in two overlapping ways: being sociable, friendly, gregarious and talkative and also being energetic and optimistic. As with Neuroticism, differences in people's Extraversion are accompanied by similar rank-order differences in their global happiness in particular settings. Once again, this intercorrelation comes about partly because some items in Extraversion questionnaires are similar to those in happiness questionnaires, but also because more extraverted people are likely to look out for extraversion-related opportunities and to move into situations that can fit with their typical preferences.[9]

Researchers have also looked at the overlap between happiness and the Big Five personality factors of Openness to Experience and Agreeableness. *Openness to Experience* covers 'thinking' interests, either an artistic orientation or a more general intellectual emphasis on conceptual and abstract topics. *Agreeableness* brings together interpersonal features such as cooperativeness, trustworthiness, sympathy and consideration for other people's wishes. Those two traits are modestly associated with happiness, much less strongly than are others in this section.

The fifth Big Five factor, *Conscientiousness*, concerns two themes associated with getting things done: first in terms of achievement motivation, striving and a determination to reach goals, and second as personal dependability, a concern for order and an acceptance of routines and authority. Those two aspects tend to go together and have usually been studied as a single factor, which is again positively correlated with measured happiness.[10]

In addition to these Big Five factors, other aspects of personality are also known to be associated with wellbeing. For example, the general trait of dispositional optimism (generally expecting positive outcomes in life) is linked to hedonic wellbeing in many situations,[11] and trait proactivity (making suggestions, showing initiative, etc.) has been shown to be associated with life satisfaction and positive affect.[12] Fewer studies have asked about links between personality and flourishing (rather than hedonic) wellbeing, but it appears that the Big Five factors of extraversion and conscientiousness are associated with a stronger purpose in life and greater self-acceptance.[13]

In these ways, our wellbeing is partly predictable from our continuing self, so that happiness and unhappiness come from a combination of the environment and ourselves.

Value priorities

Also important for happiness are people's values – their likes and dislikes about current or possible situations, activities, things or people. Sometimes described as 'conceptions of the desirable', values contribute to our feelings by influencing the content and priority of thoughts and actions. They make us more sensitive or less sensitive to different stimuli, encourage entry into different situations and modify the allocation of effort.[14] In some cases, values are within moral, religious or social codes, but they often represent individual preferences – what a person prefers, seeks and so on. They range from short-term preferences, which can vary from time to time, to longer-term orientations perhaps within a personality trait.

Each person finds some role activities more attractive than others, valuing those more positively, and particular activities can be valued in different ways by different people or by the same person at different times. Furthermore, if something matters to you, its presence or absence more strongly determines your feelings. A great deal of research has confirmed that associations between a job feature and happiness are stronger for people who more value that feature.[15] As a result, different people (with different values) can sometimes feel differently about the same environmental feature – its presence or absence matters more when it's more strongly valued.

Degree of adaptation

Your happiness also depends on your degree of adaptation. Getting 'used to' something can affect your reactions in a very short period and also across months or years, as feelings in response to a constant or repeated stimulus gradually become less pronounced or even give way to indifference. For example, a review from 313 samples confirmed positive or negative changes in wellbeing after marriage, divorce, bereavement, childbirth, unemployment, re-employment and retirement, but also demonstrated the impact of adaptation. Although the studied events were initially harmful or beneficial as expected (for instance, a clear 'honeymoon effect' was seen after marriage), subjective wellbeing was found to stabilize in the following months or years and sometimes to shift back towards previous levels.[16]

Adaptation has also been shown to occur in particular settings. American researcher Ricky Griffin found that changes to improve job satisfaction had an initially positive impact, but in two different studies average wellbeing returned to its original level after two or three years.[17] Another American study showed that job satisfaction increased immediately after managers' self-chosen move into a new position, but in subsequent years it declined significantly as people became adapted to their new role.[18] Findings of this kind have suggested the presence of a personal set point to which people return after a period of unusual stimulation – an 'equilibrium state'[19] or more likely an 'equilibrium range' of personal happiness or unhappiness.[20] We all have our own typical range of wellbeing that is stable across time and differs from many other people.

Adaptation may be viewed in terms of a raised comparison level, when exposure to earlier stimuli establishes a higher standard against which later stimuli are judged. Over time, instances of a particular stimulus have to exceed that raised comparison level in order to affect wellbeing to the same degree. Building on these themes, American psychologist Sonja Lyubomirsky (2013) explored what she termed 'the myths of happiness' in respect of ten adult 'crisis points' in personal relationships, income generation, paid jobs and ageing. She illustrated 'what should make you happy, but doesn't' in terms primarily of adaptation to personal success. Despite widespread expectations, positive occurrences do not give rise to continuing high wellbeing, since each attainment is followed by adaptation to what becomes 'the new normal'.

SHORTER-TERM PERSONAL SOURCES OF HAPPINESS: EMOTION REGULATION

So far in this chapter, we've considered some ways in which happiness is based on our longer-term personality and other characteristics. It is also shaped more proximally by our thoughts and interpretations in a current situation, and these will be reviewed next.

Research into these processes, widely described as forms of 'emotion regulation', has pointed to several thoughts and activities that might be undertaken to reduce unpleasant feelings or to enhance positive emotions. As described by American psychologist James Gross (1998, p. 275), 'emotion regulation refers to the processes by which individuals influence which emotions they have, when they have them, and how they experience and express those emotions. Emotion regulatory processes may be automatic or controlled, conscious or unconscious, and may have their effects at one or more points in the emotion generative process'.[21]

Gross's model of emotion regulation extends across five stages in which happiness might be influenced by people themselves: situation selection, situation modification, attention deployment, reappraisal and behavioural adjustment. Each of those needs to be included among the personal contributors to happiness.[22]

Situation selection and situation modification

In respect to the first two stages, we don't need scientific research to tell us that happiness can be greatly influenced by choosing which situations to enter or leave or by making positive changes to the situations we're in; that's obvious in our everyday life.

Aspects of both the selection and modification of situations can be viewed in terms of Equity Theory – expecting that people in general tend to seek relationships with other people that are perceived as fair. Within a preference for approximately equal give-and-take, studies have shown that people are likely to reciprocate others' level of contribution: if other individuals provide you with personal support, you're likely to try to support them in return.

Separate research into modification processes has focussed on 'job crafting' – the ways in which people adjust their demands or social interactions at work in order to decrease negative experiences and increase positive ones. Unsurprisingly, workers who report substantial modification of this kind are also likely to experience more job satisfaction and job engagement. They have shaped their activities to benefit their happiness.

Attention deployment

Another important form of emotion-regulation concerns how people allocate attention, directing their thoughts to one particular target rather than to others. We can often adjust our feelings by shifting mental focus to alternative themes. The 'power of positive thinking' and the benefits of 'accentuating the positive' and 'looking on the bright side' have consistently been advocated. Popular culture has long urged an optimistic shift of that kind, as in Jerome Kern's 1920 song,

> A heart full of joy and gladness
> Will always banish sadness and strife.
> So always look for the silver lining,
> And try to find the sunny side of life.

More recently, psychologists have carried out experimental studies, comparing the happiness of people who have been asked to think and behave in different ways. These have pointed to the benefits of several activities for enhancing happiness. For instance, people have been asked to think about and write down five things, once a week or once a day, about which they are grateful, and their average happiness compared against a control group doing different things. Expressing gratitude has consistently been found to increase wellbeing, as have changes to reflect on positive experiences, to express forgiveness and to practise optimism.[23]

In the same vein, research has shown that mentally detaching yourself during the evening from problems at work can aid wellbeing as you direct attention to non-job aspects of life.[24] Some studies have examined negative attention shifts that are frequently repeated – often described as 'rumination'. That recurring form of harmful attention-focus is linked to negative feelings and symptoms of depression, and it's clear that attention deployment to cut down rumination can benefit subjective wellbeing.

Other attention-deployment processes include mental comparisons between your present situation and those in the past or in a potential future – thinking how things have been getting better or worse or are likely to get better or get worse. For example, if you are able to focus attention on previous improvements or on probable future improvements, you are likely to feel more positive about your situation. Conversely, when you think about how things are getting worse or are likely to remain bad, you will probably feel worse. Those negative thoughts can sometimes include anticipatory worry about future problems. The key point is that happiness and unhappiness are not determined only by a current situation, but also from mental comparisons with how things have been previously and how they are expected to be in the future.

Two other mental comparisons are also important – against the frame of reference provided by other people and by other situations. These have both been viewed as either 'upward' or 'downward'. Emotion regulation by comparison upwards with other people involves viewing yourself against individuals who have been more successful or are in a better situation; upward comparisons have frequently been found to depress wellbeing as you see how other people are in better positions. On the other hand, downward comparisons, against people who are worse off in the compared respect, tend to encourage happiness.[25] A widespread comparison of this kind, often through the internet, is in terms of body image – how your physical appearance is thought to be more attractive or less attractive than other people's.[26]

Similarly, comparisons against other situations can shape your feelings. 'Upward' thoughts involve reflecting how things might have developed more pleasingly, and those are known to depress current wellbeing, whereas downward comparisons (considering how matters could have turned out worse than they are) can evoke more positive feelings. These two have been illustrated in a study of Olympic medallists. Runners who received silver medals for achieving second place tended to be less happy with their position than were bronze medallists in third place. Many second-place winners appeared to base their feelings in part on upward counterfactual comparisons ('I couldn't be the best'), whereas athletes in third place were more likely to make downward comparisons, being pleased to have reached the medal positions ('I did better than almost everyone').[27]

These kinds of comparative assessment have sometimes been incorporated within Equity Theory. For instance, satisfaction with your level of pay has been shown to depend on perceived comparisons with other people's pay relative to their effort, skill and other inputs. Two economists[28] have developed this idea by computing for each worker a reference level of comparison income in terms of the average amount received by others with similar occupational and demographic characteristics. Job satisfaction was found to be more strongly related to the reference level based on comparable people's income than to the actual amount that the person received. In sum, several forms of attention deployment are known to affect how happy we feel, and we have some conscious control of how we direct our thoughts.

Reappraisal

Emotion regulation also ranges across other ways in which people adjust how they think about a situation. Particularly important is the degree to which our appraisal can identify positive meanings. As concluded in a recent research review, 'a key to elevated, sustainable happiness is commitment to meaningful challenges or passions that accord with a person's self-concept and valued life domains'.[29] It's important to people that (at least sometimes) they're doing something that matters to them. Striving towards a goal can have associated benefits – leading to additional social contacts, the acquisition of new skills and knowledge, new settings for enjoyment and at least intermittently an enhanced sense of self-efficacy. And goal achievement often requires working through a succession of smaller subgoals. Positive feelings associated with attaining these intermediate targets can ensure that even unpleasant activity can generate happiness from time to time.

The personal value of responding to challenge has long been noted by non-psychologists. For instance, Scottish philosopher Adam Ferguson (1767/1966) emphasized that happiness comes primarily from being actively engaged against adversity, when people are 'placed in the middle of difficulties and obliged to employ the powers they possess' (p. 44); 'the most animating occasions of human life are calls to danger and hardship, not invitations to safety and ease' (p. 45). In that vein, people sometimes view moving to a different job in terms of 'seeking a new challenge', and researchers have found that moderately increasing the demands in your job can be a particularly powerful way for job crafting to enhance subjective wellbeing. In summary, people in the same situation can differ in how far they perceive required actions as personally meaningful, and perceived meaning is important for happiness.

Another form of reappraisal has been described as 'acceptance' – recognizing the negative aspects of a fact but mentally setting aside those unpleasant aspects. Subjective wellbeing can be improved by detaching negative feelings about a happiness-reducing fact from mere awareness of that fact – being willing and able to experience undesirable thoughts without trying to influence them and without letting them determine what you do. Global wellbeing and job satisfaction have been found to be more positive among workers who score higher on acceptance thinking,[30] and a day's negative events can be less disturbing to people who can accept those events without also experiencing associated unhappiness.[31] Mental acceptance is important here because – like other forms of emotion regulation – differences between people's thoughts about the same situation can make them happy or unhappy to different degrees.

Adjusting your behaviour

A final aspect of emotion-regulation concerns the ways in which people respond to what has happened. For example, an unhappy person might take comfort from munching through a plateful of cakes or try to improve wellbeing through exercise or meditation. Other people try to reduce their negative feelings by using alcohol or drugs.

Researchers in this area have often emphasized 'expressive suppression' – modifying behaviour by hiding how you feel. Processes of that kind have been studied in roles with a strong emphasis on service relationships, for example, when working as a server in a restaurant or a telephonist in a call centre. Interactions with rude or aggressive customers can be upsetting or annoying, and workers are often expected to conceal their negative feelings; they may be required by their organization's 'display rules' to act as though an offensive customer has behaved in an acceptable fashion. For example, an established questionnaire includes suppression items like 'I control my emotions by not expressing them' and 'I keep my emotions to myself'.[32] That form of emotional suppression has been found to be linked with psychological strain, emotional exhaustion, low job satisfaction and similar forms of unhappiness.[33]

In review of this section, forms of emotion regulation are among the foundations of personal happiness.[34] They operate to shape how life is experienced, and they're often part of long-established habits of thinking. Single instances of regulation can derive from mental and behavioural routines that have become established as habits through many years of repetition, and in many cases the habits form part of a personality trait.

ASSOCIATIONS BETWEEN LONGER-TERM AND SHORTER-TERM PERSONAL SOURCES

We've so far looked separately at longer-term and shorter-term personal influences on happiness and now need to examine the overlaps between them. However, studies that bring together the two levels are rare. Here are some examples.

In respect to age, older people have been found to be more effective in managing their emotions and more likely to regulate their wellbeing by accepting what happens to them rather than being troubled by associated negative feelings.[35] People with personalities that are more Neurotic look out for worrying possibilities in many situations, often seeing threats and possible dangers in the world around them. Neurotic individuals are more likely to think of reasons to be unhappy, expecting unhappiness as their default position. Similarly, extraverted people often think differently from those who are introverted, for instance, more frequently making 'downward' social comparisons – noticing more than introverts when other people's situations are worse than their own. As we've seen, mental comparisons of a downward kind are generally likely to aid happiness.

Long-term traits like self-esteem are similarly reflected in emotion regulation in particular situations. People with consistently low self-esteem tend more than others to make upward social and counterfactual comparisons, those that are likely to sustain their low self-esteem.[36] Other long-term traits are also known to be important in some forms of short-term regulation; for instance, proactivity is linked to situation modification through job crafting.[37] And when an activity is more valued, it's particularly likely to affect happiness in particular settings. Long- and short-term personal contributors can in these ways work together to yield happiness or unhappiness, but once again we need more research.

THE ENVIRONMENT AND THE PERSON: 'SITUATIONAL STRENGTH'

What about the relative importance for happiness of environmental features and personal processes? A standard pattern of environment-versus-person impact is not likely since the two kinds of feature can vary in their relative intensity. For instance, a particularly powerful input such as one that is extremely painful can take precedence over other features. Examining the relative contribution of the person and the environment on particular behaviours, American researcher Walter Mischel developed the notion of 'situational strength', a situation's potential to take priority over personal variables.[38] This has, for example, been examined through comparisons between 'strong' and 'weak' jobs.

'Weaker' situations are less structured and permit more personal discretion and freedom of action, whereas settings that are 'strong' more limit behaviours by requiring people to operate within narrow restrictions. Influences from the person have been found to be more important for job behaviour and wellbeing in 'weak' conditions, whereas the environment more strongly influences those outcomes in 'strong' situations.[39] So the relative significance of the person versus the environment is known to depend on characteristics of the situation and the person under investigation; there is not a universal pattern of relative impact. Additional studies and theorizing in this area are now greatly needed.

CHAPTER 5: SOME TAKE-HOME MESSAGES

Inputs from the environment around us are not the entire basis of happiness or unhappiness; we must also consider the influence of personal characteristics and processes. Research has pointed to the importance for subjective wellbeing of longer-term characteristics such as age, gender and personality and to the overarching importance of genetic factors. Within specific situations, several processes of emotion regulation have been shown to affect happiness, such as people's choice of settings to enter or leave, the way they direct their attention and how they appraise what is happening to them. These shorter-term processes often reflect habits that have become established over many years.

6

SOME CONSEQUENCES OF HAPPINESS

Previous chapters have looked at different kinds of happiness and their sources – in the world and in people themselves. We should also consider possible consequences – the actions and thoughts that can flow from feeling good or feeling bad.[1] Drawing from a large number of studies, Sonja Lyubomirsky, Laura Wing and Ed Diener[2] in 2005 identified significant associations with six kinds of behaviour.

Sociability and activity level: Happy individuals have frequently been found to be more sociable than others, with higher levels of social interaction, activity and energy; research has frequently indicated that happiness goes along with being involved in projects with other people and being engaged in the world around you.

Volunteering to help other people: The 2005 review also demonstrated that providing help to other people (sometimes called 'citizenship' or 'prosocial' behaviour) is more likely among happier individuals; better wellbeing is associated with more social contributions.

Positive perceptions, memories and predictions: Happy people also view other people and themselves in more favourable terms, with more positive attitudes to situations and people in their life. Within that positive bias, they tend to have more cheerful recollections, and they make more optimistic predictions about the future.

Likeability and attractiveness: The 2005 review also summarized findings that happy individuals are rated as more friendly, socially skilled, competent, intelligent, physically attractive and less selfish than others.

Health behaviours and condition: Differences in health behaviours have also been found. For example, people who more abuse drugs and alcohol, smoke or eat excessively tend to be less happy than others. In addition, hedonic happiness has often found to accompany more positive self-reports of health. (A later section will look in more detail at health-related possibilities.)

Creativity and problem-solving: Finally, the 2005 review suggested (but evidence was less strong) that people who are more happy might be more flexible, creative and effective at problem-solving.

That and other reviews do not distinguish between different scopes of happiness, for example, between feature-specific and global happiness. Recalling that happiness is usually 'about' or 'with' something, we might expect stronger associations with behaviour when happiness scope is narrow, for example, about individual features such as your house, your neighbour and so on. Feature-specific happiness comes close to what has been studied as an attitude, and attitudes (often identified as having a 'behavioural component') are by definition expected to influence conceptually linked behaviours. An analysis of 88 previous investigations[3] confirmed that people's attitudes were indeed significantly correlated with their subsequent behaviours – adhering to a diet, discriminating racially, voting for political parties, driving rapidly and so on. In a similar way, workers' job wellbeing is moderately associated with their job performance.[4]

In summary, the 2005 review and other publications have made it clear that happiness (especially when narrowly focussed) is associated with a range of behaviours and thoughts. However, it's well-known that causation cannot be inferred from a correlation. Four different causal interpretations are possible when a significant correlation is found between happiness and a behaviour:

- Happiness causes the behaviour.
- The behaviour causes happiness.
- Happiness and the behaviour cause each other.
- One or more additional variables cause both happiness and the behaviour.

Several of these possibilities may operate together, but it's useful to review them one by one. The first interpretation (happiness causes the behaviour) is straightforward and widely expected, illustrated in an advertising slogan from earlier years – 'contented cows produce the best milk'. For example, happiness might lead people to be more interested in their environment, sympathetic to other people and generally more active.

Second, causation might be in the reverse direction, as behaviour causes an increase in happiness. That could occur because a behaviour modifies some of the desirable features in Chapter 4, leading indirectly to increased happiness. For example, actions to bring about greater personal control over the environment (feature one) or more extensive skill utilization (feature two) can lead to increased happiness. In a job setting, effective performance might lead to increased pay (feature seven) and associated benefits to wellbeing.

The third possible interpretation of a significant correlation between happiness and a behaviour is that those two processes might both be important. Happiness might generate behaviour (as suggested by possibility one) and may also be a response to previous goal achievement, effectiveness and associated personal rewards (possibility two).

A few publications have examined longitudinal associations across time: is happiness followed by behaviour of a certain kind, or does the behaviour precede happiness? The general finding is that that lagged patterns (the ones across time) are similar to but sometimes smaller than cross-sectional associations.[5] However, even when increased subjective wellbeing has been shown to occur before enhanced performance, causal impact from wellbeing cannot be inferred. Rank-order differences between many personal characteristics tend to be maintained across fairly lengthy periods of time, as different people continue to behave and feel in much the same rank order so that a later measurement in part reflects an earlier state. People's rank order doesn't change very much. Given that later measures can also reflect earlier ones, a lagged correlation is similar to one that is cross-sectional and may reflect causal influence in either direction. So longitudinal correlations are also causally ambiguous.

Finally, the fourth causal process deserves particular attention. A significant correlation might arise because one or more *additional* variables cause both happiness and the studied behaviour – sometimes said to reflect the impact of 'third variables'. For example, background features (such as better living conditions or help from friends) might generate both happiness and a particular kind of behaviour. Extended impacts on happiness-behaviour correlations are also expected from third variables in the form of continuing personality traits, such that (for instance) extraverted individuals across time both feel more happy and behave in ways that differ from more introverted people; the trait of extraversion might causally affect both a person's happiness and a particular behaviour rather than one of those causing the other. Despite researchers' statistical control of some possible 'third variables' such as age and gender, we can often think of features in the environment or the person that might be causally important but have been omitted from an investigation. It is essential to check out those additional possibilities.

LABORATORY EXPERIMENTS TO MODIFY HAPPINESS

Against that uncertain background, some researchers into the impact of happiness have turned to laboratory experiments in which situations or instructions modify feelings in a positive or negative direction. Happiness has been manipulated in these experiments by asking people to watch a cheerful film clip, giving them an unexpected small gift, reading about positive occurrences or being exposed to an attractive scent. Limited procedures of that kind have proved to be successful in the short term, often in samples of university students divided into groups such that different groups receive different happiness treatments.

Laboratory experiments have obtained consistent findings when comparing the consequences of induced positive affect versus neutral conditions, but of course those findings might not be generalizable to real-life settings. Everyday life is much more complex and includes many additional variables and social processes. Furthermore, induced happiness in the laboratory is unlikely to endure beyond about 20 minutes, and everyday activities often generate sequences of experiences that shuttle to and fro across several days between negative and positive. Nevertheless, although laboratory findings can't be directly applied to everyday life, experimental observations together with repeated personal experience suggest to many people that changes in happiness do have some influence on thoughts and behaviour.

Global happiness comes largely from the accumulation of more-focussed feelings in earlier periods. This means that short-term feelings are especially important as they combine with other feelings into broader-scope, longer-duration happiness. So maybe briefly experienced happiness in the laboratory has some relevance to everyday life. Let's take a look at findings in two areas – people's thought processes and their interactions with others.

Studying thought processes in the laboratory

The induction of mild positive affect has been shown to affect thoughts in several ways. It leads to more positive perceptions, improves the recall of positive material and gives rise to more positive judgements about neutral material.[6] For instance, increased positive affect has been shown in the laboratory to give rise to significantly more wide-ranging mental processes, more positive judgements about neutral material, greater persistence and enhanced optimism. In respect of productive performance, a laboratory comparison of arithmetic calculations found that the output of participants with induced positive mood exceeded control groups by an average of 12 per cent.[7]

Positive priming has also been shown for judgements of expectancy – happy individuals tend to think that positive outcomes are more likely. That's important in respect of differences in motivation, which can sometimes depend on whether you expect an action to successfully produce the desired outcome. After positive mood induction, expectancies tend to be higher than in control groups, and people are more optimistic about future developments from their actions.[8]

Laboratory research has also suggested that happy people process complex information more speedily and that they adopt a wider perspective. For example, induced positive affect appears to encourage a broader attention span, whereas negative feelings lead to a narrowing of attention and perceptual focus. That was first observed in simulated flying tasks in World War Two, when pilot error in difficult activities often arose from a failure to respond to signals near the edges of a laboratory display. By restricting their attention to tasks considered to be central, people under overload strain can maintain or enhance central performance, but their effectiveness on infrequent or peripheral tasks can become impaired.

Conversely, negative affect has been found to give rise to greater attentiveness to detail, with less happy people thinking in a more analytical manner. Happier individuals are likely to base their judgements more on prior assumptions, perhaps relying on habitual expectations rather than checking and working through the entirety of new information. Induced happiness has also been shown to increase risk-taking in hypothetical situations or when the perceived probability of winning is high. As in the earlier discussion of happiness sources in Chapter 4, in terms of consequences, perhaps you can also have 'too much of a good thing'. Although moderate levels of happiness can be valuable, positive affect at a very high level can lead to carelessness, over-optimism and underestimates of potential harm.

Experimental research in the laboratory has also indicated that happiness inductions can promote creativity, in terms of the elicitation of more unusual and more diverse associations to neutral stimulus words. However, real-life innovation requires more than merely creative thinking in terms of unusual associations. Problem-solving in practical settings often involves extended sequences of activity, as people work to overcome obstacles across time, perhaps in collaboration with other people – a lot more than the type of creativity examined in laboratory studies, often in terms merely of unusual mental associations.

Furthermore, creativity and other mental processes can be linked to feelings that are negative. Innovation is often provoked by external pressure, as in the suggestion that 'necessity is the mother of invention'. In those cases, negative events can disrupt current performance and create unhappiness but also generate novel solutions; adverse circumstances may thus reduce happiness but promote creativity. Once again, we need to consider possible 'third variables': rather than unhappiness alone being the cause of a creative solution, it's the need for change that leads to creative behaviour.

Studying social relations in the laboratory

Other laboratory studies have asked about sociability, helpfulness, generosity and cooperativeness. Findings are clear that those forms of interpersonal interaction are all likely to increase after the laboratory induction of happiness, as research participants become more attracted to making connections with others. Social interaction is perceived as more desirable when people are happy, and happy people are more likely to expect good developments from social encounters.

In some cases, happiness can influence behaviour through contributions from other people rather than entirely on your own. As outlined earlier, our willingness to help others (which is itself promoted by more positive feelings) is often linked to the receipt of social support in return – a process of reciprocity. Given that happy individuals tend more to help others, it is sometimes likely that their subsequent happiness derives in part from the reciprocal support received from other people.

SOME MODERATING INFLUENCES

So far, we've looked at average patterns across groups of people, but of course some differences occur around those averages. We need also to look into possible moderators – aspects of the situation or person that can account for differences in the size of correlations between happiness and behaviour.

Early research in this area focussed on the constraints limiting versus permitting personal discretion. In some situations, we are relatively free to decide how things should be done, but in other settings external restrictions more enforce particular kinds of behaviour. Those constraints might derive from organizational or national regulations, an absence of other possibilities, decision-making by a machine or strong social norms. When external constraints are strong, personal variables such as happiness are likely to have a reduced impact on behaviour.

As outlined in the last chapter, the continuum between external and internal influences on behaviour was viewed by Walter Mischel in terms of 'situational strength'. A principal component of this is the degree to which a setting acts to constrain possible behaviours. Situations of high constraint – 'strong' in Mischel's account – reduce your opportunity for discretion and personal influence, as behaviour becomes more determined by the environment. Systematic reviews of previous investigations have shown that happiness is more strongly associated with behaviour when situations impose fewer constraints on personal autonomy.[9] For instance, situations with considerable opportunity for personal discretion, as in confidential voting, are particularly influenced by feelings towards each candidate. It's clear that differences between situational strength are important moderating determinants of the correlation between happiness and behaviour.[10]

Differences in discretion have sometimes been considered by work psychologists in terms of organizational grade. Managers and professional staff have more freedom than others to determine their own activities, so it may be that correlations between wellbeing and work performance will be greater among managerial staff than among lower-grade workers. Early investigations supported that possibility, but it has rarely been examined in recent years.

Social pressures provide another constraint on discretionary behaviour, through the operation of strong group norms about which behaviours are acceptable or unacceptable. In cases where a group has established a normatively prescribed way of behaving, it may be that a person's own happiness will less determine actions than in the absence of a socially-approved behaviour. Early research in this area emphasized that work-group cohesiveness is likely to promote norms of either low or high productivity, with reduced opportunity in cohesive groups for an impact from happiness or other personal characteristics. Additional investigations are now needed.

Some characteristics of wellbeing itself have been shown to influence the magnitude of happiness-behaviour associations. For instance, in the few studies that examined both positive and negative indicators of affect, positive feelings have consistently been found to be more strongly associated with positive behaviour than negative feelings. In addition, the activation level of wellbeing has a strong impact on observed correlations. Most studies have investigated feelings that are all activated, so that much of the research literature reports significant associations between wellbeing and behaviour that are in fact restricted to activated forms of wellbeing. However, recent reviews of creativity and other behaviours leave no doubt that associations with behaviour are substantially stronger with more activated positive feelings than with those which are less activated.[11] Once again, in the overworked academic phrase, 'further research is needed'.

WHAT TO CONCLUDE ABOUT CAUSE AND EFFECT?

This chapter has described two kinds of investigation into the potential consequences of happiness. In everyday settings, significant correlations have been found between happiness and certain behaviours, and laboratory comparisons have shown that inducing positive affect gives rise to positive thoughts and increased social interaction. However, both kinds of study are limited in their own way, and both are difficult to interpret in terms of cause and effect.

Recognizing that correlation doesn't indicate cause, we can't draw formal conclusions about causation from the associations recorded in everyday settings. And although laboratory experiments do show that inducing positive affect can change some behaviours and thoughts, that form of research is carried out in artificial conditions and has outcomes that are short-lived; happiness findings might not generalize beyond the laboratory. However, in everyday life short-term happiness experiences are common, serving as building blocks of longer-term wellbeing, and maybe happiness in the laboratory parallels everyday experiences in essential respects. More generally, positive feelings are associated with traits of optimism, confidence, sociability and other characteristics that encourage active involvement in the world. This means that short-term experiences of happiness can sometimes change one or more of the book's happiness-promoting features and as a result modify a situation and improve wellbeing.

So what should we conclude? Perhaps we should also look beyond formal research and purist logic to personal experiences. Everyday life suggests to many people that their feelings can sometimes determine behaviour, as they see how positive or negative moods appear to be shaping their actions. On balance, it seems that the repeatedly found correlation between happiness and behaviour does in fact reflect some causation.[12] Happiness is likely sometimes to influence behaviour, but behaviour is also caused in other ways, and causal processes are expected to vary between situations.

DOES HAPPINESS INFLUENCE YOUR PHYSICAL HEALTH?

Finally in this chapter, let's look at a question that illustrates many of the themes raised earlier. Does your happiness or unhappiness determine your state of physical health? As noted in Chapter 1, psychological wellbeing overlaps substantially with aspects of *mental* health, so we would expect people with low mental health also to be unhappy. But what about *physical* ill health? Can that be influenced by your psychological state? Might cheerfully 'looking on the bright side' make it less probable you'll become physically ill or increase an ill person's chances of getting better?

Some studies have measured physical health in terms of self-report – how well or ill you consider yourself to be – finding that people are more likely to report good health if they're happy. However, self-reported health is effectively a measure of domain-specific happiness, here in terms of happiness about your health domain, and we have seen that increasing happiness can shift perceptions to become more positive. Findings about *self-reported* health thus reflect conceptual overlap rather than a link between different variables. We need to measure ill health in objective rather than subjective terms – as medical diagnoses, hospital admissions, heart attacks and so on. Researchers who study objective indicators of that kind have found a moderate association between low happiness and later illnesses, even after a number of other possible influences (income, prior ill health, social involvement, etc.) have been statistically controlled.[13]

That is also the case for comparisons of subsequent mortality between happy and unhappy people – the age at which people die: positive feelings have in several longitudinal studies been linked to more years of future life. One prospective investigation looked at optimism (a key part of happiness) and its association with reduced mortality in older women.[14] Strong associations were found for each major cause of death: more optimistic older women were less likely to die early from cancer, heart disease, stroke, respiratory disease and infection. Statistical controls for demographic characteristics, health conditions and health behaviours reduced the predictive importance of optimism, but the associations were still present.

Do these findings mean that happiness causes good health or low mortality? Not definitely. For example, although optimism predicts later date of death, we need to know why some people are more optimistic than others when data are gathered. Perhaps living conditions, genes or personality traits shape pessimism or optimism and also influence how long you live. Or maybe your state of health at the time of measurement influences both your current optimism and your later mortality. In addition to happiness and related variables, we need to consider other possible causes – 'third variables' again.

In these ways, we must always consider the possibility of influences from variables that haven't been measured. For instance, minor ill health at initial measurement might be the precursor of later severe illness, and health-promoting behaviours (exercising, healthy eating, sound sleep, etc.) tend to be more frequent among happy people. Examining interpretation problems in this area, one comprehensive review concluded that 'even with statistical controls, longitudinal studies do not with certainty rule out third variable explanations of the findings. There might always be other unobserved variables that are responsible for the association'.[15] Another review concluded that, although longitudinal findings are clearer for cardiovascular problems, 'the evidence that positive subjective wellbeing helps those with diseases such as cancer appears to be mixed, with uncertain overall support at the present time'.[16]

In summary, although positive correlations between happiness and health have often been significant, we should be cautious about the possible causal importance of happiness. A direct causal role for happiness in relation to objective physical health or subsequent mortality has yet to be confirmed.

CHAPTER 6: SOME TAKE-HOME MESSAGES

Happiness is linked with more positive thinking and greater sociability both in daily life and in laboratory experiments. However, extremely positive feelings can lead to carelessness and limited attention to detail; for happiness, we can again 'have too much of a good thing'. Its likely impact on behaviour varies between circumstances, in particular between different levels of personal discretion. In general, happiness predicts health-promoting behaviours, health that is self-reported, some illnesses and people's age of death, but it's unclear whether it is directly influential or whether other causal mechanisms might be more important.

7

WHAT TO DO NOW?

This final chapter is in two parts. First it looks at possible ways to improve your happiness, drawing on ideas from earlier in the book. The second section is more specialized, aimed at psychology researchers and students, and many readers will choose to omit that.

PART 1: CAN YOU IMPROVE YOUR HAPPINESS?

Much of life is the product of habits developed across many years, and habits repeated over and over again are difficult to change. As part of that general pattern, each person's happiness is partly based on habits of behaviour and of thinking – often long-established and firmly entrenched. Some improvements might be possible, but don't expect big changes overnight. Instead it's often best to aim for a succession of small improvements.

Research has confirmed that even usually happy individuals have times when they are anything but happy. People may become upset about their children, worried about their amateur dramatic performance or unhappy about their partner; short-term unhappiness is part of life. In the same way, it's common to have mixed feelings about a situation, either because you feel differently about its different aspects or because your enjoyment varies from time to time. So you can be unhappy about your life at the present moment for all sorts of reasons, but you can still overall be positive about it.

In this section we need to focus on the medium term, without being swayed too much by a temporary good or bad mood. So for the first section of this chapter, let's look beyond the immediate present to think in terms of happiness in recent weeks or months. Suggestions will be offered in respect of three different themes. First, it's important to review your level and kinds of happiness or unhappiness. Then consider what might be done to improve your situation. And third, look at adjusting your own behaviours and styles of thinking.

Theme 1: look at your happiness

The book has emphasized that there are many kinds of happiness and unhappiness. As described in Chapters 1 and 2, most discussions have been about hedonic happiness rather than about flourishing, so we might concentrate on that. An initial question is about feelings as a whole, for instance, 'How satisfied are you with your life in general?' Think about that first, perhaps on a scale from 'I'm extremely dissatisfied' through 'slightly dissatisfied' and 'about OK' to 'slightly satisfied' and 'extremely satisfied'. If your life satisfaction seems less than is desirable, you need to look in more detail at specific feelings in terms of Figure 2.1 on page 11.

You may remember that this diagram brings together different feelings in terms of their valence and activation, such that they can be summarized both as pleasing or displeasing and also as more activated or less activated.[1] In those terms, happiness or unhappiness can be summarized in terms of four general types, labelled here as Enthusiasm (cheerful, excited, etc. – positive, activated feelings), Comfort (contented, relaxed, etc. – positive and less activated), Anxiety (afraid, tense, etc. – negative and activated) and Depression (miserable, gloomy, etc. – negative and less activated). Remember, it's not unusual to have feelings that are both negative and positive; many people live with some unpleasant aspects in their world, recognizing that those are at least outweighed by positive themes.

The left-hand sections of Figure 2.1 identify two ways in which you can feel bad – through Anxiety or Depression. Anxious feelings include tension and worry, but depression is a question of feeling gloomy or miserable. Is your unhappiness more a question of Anxiety or Depression?[2] Different kinds of feeling are likely to occur in different circumstances: the anxious form of unhappiness (top left in Figure 2.1) usually comes from overload or personal threat, whereas depression (bottom left) comes more from a loss or a low level of a desirable feature or from a failure to achieve personal goals.

For example, many people struggle with high levels of anxiety because of combined excessive demands from home, family, a job and their voluntary or social commitments, whereas others are depressed by loss – the death of a parent or partner or the breakdown of a relationship. Of course, some negative feelings are unavoidable as you tackle problems and face difficulties in your life, so we need to ask whether they are intensely negative or merely slightly negative. How do you feel in that respect? In cases of great unhappiness, you should next review the nature of your situation.

Theme 2: look at your situation

Assuming that your feelings are more negative than you'd like, we now have to ask why that has happened and whether it's likely to continue in the future. We'll need to look at your situation and also at yourself. First, your situation – what is happening in your world? That can usefully be considered in terms of the happiness-affecting features from Chapter 4. Here they are again:

1 Personal influence – being able to affect what happens
2 Using your abilities – applying your skills
3 Demands and goals – what you have to do
4 Variety – different activities
5 Clear requirements and outlook – not too much uncertainty
6 Contacts with other people – enough and good dealings with others

7 Money – at least enough to live on
8 Adequate physical setting – housing, equipment, etc.
9 A valued role – doing something felt to be worthwhile

Each feature can take many different forms, and some of those may be more relevant or less relevant to you. For example, high levels of demands and goals (feature 3) might include caring for children or parents, pressures from your job, work-home conflict and a large number of social commitments, as well as demands arising from other features in the list.

Are any of the happiness-affecting features or their subcomponents particularly troubling you? Recall that the first six of them can be excessive – you can have too much of them. One possibility is to think in terms of a scale from 'very much too low' through 'much too low', 'slightly too low' and 'acceptable' to 'slightly too high', 'much too high' and 'very much too high'. Do you rate any aspects within a happiness-affecting feature as excessively low or high? If that's the case, something needs attention. You might want to work on the one that is most troubling you, the biggest issue. Or you could start by picking one or two small problems that seem to be potentially soluble – trying to sort those out before moving on to the more difficult issues.

In parallel with a feature-by-feature approach to increasing happiness, it's important also to take a broader look at your life. Happiness can be thought of in terms of what American psychologist Tal Ben-Shahar has described as the 'MPS process' – concerned with 'meaning', 'pleasure' and 'strengths'. He suggests you ask three questions: 'What gives me meaning in my life? In other words, what provides me with a sense of purpose?', 'What gives me pleasure? In other words, what do I enjoy doing?' and 'What are my strengths? In other words, what am I good at?'[3] You may have noticed that 'meaning' here brings in aspects of flourishing wellbeing introduced in Chapter 3, 'pleasure' extends across hedonic wellbeing (Chapter 2) and 'strengths' overlap with personal values (Chapter 5).

To increase happiness, Ben-Shahar urges us to look beyond merely the 'pleasure' aspects (the ones you enjoy) and try to maximize all three aspects. Can you identify areas where you could build on your situation's potential for 'meaning' and where you can better exploit your strengths? The latter have been brought together by University of Pennsylvania professors Martin Seligman and Christopher Peterson into 24 'signature strengths' – the ones that are particularly yours.[4] Grouped into six broad categories, the strengths are:

- Wisdom and Knowledge: creativity, curiosity, judgement, love of learning, perspective
- Courage: bravery, persistence, honesty, zest
- Humanity: love, kindness, social intelligence
- Justice: teamwork, fairness, leadership
- Temperance: forgiveness, humility, prudence, self-regulation
- Transcendence: appreciation of beauty and excellence, gratitude, hope, humour, spirituality

Given that activities based on our signature strengths are good for our happiness, it's worth aiming to adjust parts of your life to find a way to use them more than before. For example, if learning is 'your thing', you might spend more time finding out about topics that interest you; and if you're strong on kindness a role helping others would be good for you.

It's also a good idea to focus the MPS or signature-strength framework onto each of the nine happiness-affecting features described here – personal influence, using your abilities and so on. Some of those will probably be OK, so that problems are restricted to only a few aspects. Can those be improved in terms of meaning, pleasure and using your strengths? How can you do that?

Of course, a single, universal solution to the many possible problems is out of the question. Situations can be troublesome in many different ways, and a brief section in the final chapter of a small book can't possibly suggest how to handle all the difficulties you might face. However, if you're going to make things happen, you have to *really want* to make an effort and persist with that despite inevitable difficulties. It can be useful to talk with other people who are not directly

involved or might be able to help out. They may have their own suggestions, and anyway it's often comforting to be among friends.

Theme 3: look at yourself

Although the nine happiness features are crucial for people in general, of course we're not all the same. Chapter 5 has described how
two personal aspects are also important for happiness – long-term
characteristics like traits of personality, and processes of appraisal and
interpretation in particular situations. For example, we all have typical
levels of generally positive or negative feelings about things, and our
reactions to events are shaped by this general affective outlook. If
you're typically a cheerful person, the odds are you'll be more cheerful than many others wherever you are, and conversely people with
a more negative outlook will in almost any conditions be less happy
than others.

As we've also seen, across a period of time everyone is likely to
move back towards a personal happiness baseline. So you must ask
yourself: would I feel happier in a few months' time if certain changes
to my situation were made now, or am I instead likely after a while
to feel much as I do at present? A crucial factor is of course the magnitude of change: something that is hugely different from now can
have a continuing effect on you, but the benefits from a small or
moderate change probably won't last long. It's often helpful to reflect
about a previous similar change. How long did the impact last? Was
the duration long enough to be worth the hassle that went into making the change?

That point may seem a bit negative: surely we should keep striving
to make things better for ourselves and our family, even if we'll even-
tually slip back towards our previous feelings? Well, yes, we certainly
should, but it's important to be realistic. One alternative is to live with
something that is OK but less than perfect, recognizing that much of
life is like that. You can cause yourself a great deal of difficulty and
anxiety trying to alter central aspects of your life, only to find that a
minor change doesn't much alter your happiness in the longer term.

Feelings are unlikely to shift enormously across an extended period unless changes in a situation have been substantial and continuing.

Let's look again at the basic question: are you unhappy enough to want to try to do something about it? In the light of your personality and happiness baseline, this now becomes: recognizing that you are likely to return towards your happiness baseline after a while, are you unhappy enough to want to try to do something about it? You may sometimes feel it's best to accept what you've got. However, another kind of change may be possible and helpful: rather than trying to change your situation, maybe you could alter your ways of thinking. Even better, could you do both – modify aspects of your world and also adjust some styles of thinking? Let's think about what you might do.

Chapter 5 showed how happiness is in part due to how you interpret and process what happens to you. Two people in the same situation can feel differently about it. Forms of emotion regulation – such as directing your attention in particular directions, comparing yourself favourably with other people and accepting some negative aspects – can all influence your feelings and can deserve attention here. Do you often think along lines that are likely to make you feel less happy than you might be?

It's sometimes difficult to analyze yourself in that way, and here are three suggestions that might point you to make improvements. First, pause in the course of some future negative episodes and reflect about your thought processes. What sort of mental comparisons have you made against other people and other situations? How high were your expectations, and how realistic do you now believe them to have been? Would alternative interpretations along the lines of Chapter 5 have made a difference to your happiness?

Second, you could think back to a recent unpleasant event. How did you view that as you reacted to it? For instance, did you bring to mind the good things you'll be missing or think about other people who didn't have your misfortune? Those comparisons (called 'upward' in earlier chapters) serve to emphasize your own relative lack of success and are likely to depress your mood.

Third, it's a good idea sometimes to watch and listen to other people in your life: how do they think and react in unpleasant situations? Are they making upward or downward comparisons? Do their mental spectacles lead them to think in more positive ways than you do?

Overall then, given that both your personal baseline and your thinking styles can affect your happiness or unhappiness, you may need to consider possible ways to change those aspects of yourself. Can you do anything to alter the way you view the world, even if you can't change the world itself? It's not easy to modify your long-term characteristics and habits, but you might be able to alter some particular behaviours and thoughts that underlie them. For instance, people with high scores on Neuroticism scales – indicating an entrenched habit to think negatively – are likely in many situations to spend time looking for problems and ruminating about possible reasons and solutions; they may inappropriately blame themselves when things go wrong. Such thinking styles clearly need attention.

Try identifying and stopping negative thoughts as soon as they start. Even better, aim to replace them with ideas that are positive: maybe that project did go wrong, but your involvement was good because things could have become a lot worse without you. Generally, try to shift negative kinds of thinking into other channels, for instance, more readily accepting hassles without dwelling on them too much. Can you identify a few kinds of your harmful thoughts that could be shifted just a little? Several are illustrated in Chapter 5. And find some more optimistic ideas that are personally meaningful for you.

As well as the negative impact of Neuroticism, Chapter 5 described how the traits of Conscientiousness and Extraversion go along with more positive feelings, so we ought also to look at behaviours within those traits. For example, setting yourself new goals (an instance of behaviour by a Conscientious personality) not only takes your mind off negative thoughts (because you're busy getting on with things) but may also lead to some enjoyable outcomes as you turn the goals into action. Similarly, increasing activities with other people (one part of being Extraverted) has often been shown to encourage happiness.

The general point is that personality traits are difficult to change in their entirety, but some of their behaviours might be adjusted to increase happiness. You may feel anxious at first in the new situations, but there's a good chance that persistence will yield rewards.

Turning to particular forms of emotion regulation, Chapter 5 identified 'upward' mental comparisons (with people or situations that are better than yours) as a common source of problems. Some people have a habit of contrasting their financial position, their physical appearance or something else against people who are clearly successful (nowadays often through internet social media), yet we know from research that these 'upward' comparisons tend to be linked with lower wellbeing. Instead, try persuading yourself to view aspects of your situation in other comparative ways: which aspects of your life are better than certain other people's, better than they used to be, better than they could be or better than you expected? Similarly, how are the bad features balanced by good ones?

In general then, you may be able to increase your happiness by adjusting some personality-linked behaviours and by modifying some thinking styles. In part, this has been described as the need to 'challenge unhelpful thoughts', perhaps using procedures drawn from short-term cognitive behaviour therapy (CBT) as provided to clinical patients with anxiety, depression and other mental illnesses. CBT is a brief 'talking' treatment, with a focus on how patients think about what happens to them and ways in which harmful thoughts may be changed.

Research has shown that tackling unhelpful thoughts can be very effective in the clinic, and similar thought-adjusting procedures can also be useful for life more generally. Typical issues in need of attention include:

- Overgeneralization: coming to an overly general negative conclusion from a single piece of evidence (e.g., 'I made a mess of that relationship. I can't ever get close to other people').
- Excessively concentrating on the negative: ignoring or downgrading positive aspects of a situation (e.g., 'I was unsuccessful in

that job interview', when you also learned a lot about which topics you should cover in future interviews and when the successful candidate was exceptionally strong).

- Believing you are widely at fault: taking responsibility for something negative that you haven't caused (e.g., 'My partner is really irritable today. I must have done something wrong' or 'I was unsuccessful because I'm no good' when the activity in question was too difficult for almost anyone).

Of course, we all veer in a negative direction from time to time, but it's hard to disagree with the suggestion that less negative thinking would mean more happiness. Try mentally challenging some of your own negative thoughts of these kinds.

There's some evidence that women more often talk to other people when they need cheering up and that men see more value in being active (for instance, in hobbies, sports and so on); also that most people – men and women – find that chatting with other people can be helpful. However, situations and problems differ widely (for instance, you might be in a situation where you don't have anyone to chat with), so it's not sensible to look for all-embracing solutions.

In recent years, psychologists have carried out experiments to learn about the different ways in which people might improve their happiness. Experimental procedures have compared wellbeing after different groups are asked to act or think in different ways. Professor Sonja Lyubomirsky of the University of California has brought together recent studies into 12 key 'happiness activities'.[5] Some illustrations are:

- Expressing gratitude and 'counting your blessings': you can sometimes feel better by writing down some aspects of your life for which you are grateful. Other activities of this kind include telling people in a face-to-face chat or in a letter that you appreciate something they have done. Have any friends or family members helped you recently? We often feel uncomfortable about making public our grateful feelings, but doing so can yield several personal benefits – emphasizing positive aspects of your life, bolstering self-esteem and perceived self-worth, and building pleasant relationships as others respond in a positive way.

- Avoiding excessive rumination about yourself and your situation. When you feel downhearted, it is certainly sensible to focus on possible reasons and solutions, but those thoughts can go too far. Research as well as common sense has shown how continued rumination can make things worse. Although life can sometimes be upsetting, it's essential to stop dwelling on particular problems and their possible causes.
- Investing in social connections, for instance through group membership: people who increase their friendly social contacts are known to become happier. There are several reasons for that. Social contact itself is needed to reduce feelings of loneliness, but in addition, discussions with other people can provide useful ideas and information as well as making comforting suggestions when you have problems. Generally, meeting with others can serve to lift your mood.

Other self-initiated happiness activities reviewed by Lyubomirsky include committing yourself to goals, learning to forgive, cultivating optimism and taking care of your body. Perhaps you could select the ones you like, and see if they are helpful. As in all cases here, the need is to embed the new style within a habit that gradually becomes part of your life, so it's essential to keep working to consolidate the new routine or you'll slip back into earlier habits.

Happiness improvement: an overview

This book has described how happiness and unhappiness derive largely from nine features in your life, but it has repeatedly emphasized that they also come from within yourself. To improve your own or someone else's happiness, it's desirable to work on possible improvements from both directions – your situation and yourself.

Needed changes to a situation obviously depend on what the problem is, but in respect of personal change, negative thoughts need to be directed into more positive themes. For some people that is extremely difficult, and none of us find it easy. A general theme is that we go through life partly on autopilot, reacting to situations through habitual routines of thought and action. Some of these routines are bad for wellbeing, and personal routine changes are worth exploring.

PART 2: HOW CAN WE DEVELOP OUR RESEARCH?

(*This final section is written primarily for academic readers, and others may prefer to omit it.*)

Some issues covered in this book have attracted many excellent investigations, but as a general field happiness has been unfashionable among academic psychologists. That means that undergraduate and graduate students have rarely been introduced to the appeal of happiness research, and so are less likely to think in those terms in their later careers.

Yet happiness and its implications are central to many popular issues in academic psychology, although − crucially − other labels and perspectives are usually applied. Themes of this book are essential to but often unrecognized in studies of motivation, reward, values, learning, job design, social influence, leadership, attitudes, personal development and many other areas. There is a major need for psychologists to apply and develop happiness constructs when investigating other issues.

With that in mind, this section is addressed to academic psychologists and their students, and 11 promising avenues for happiness research are summarized.

Incorporate happiness models into apparently unconnected research

This first suggestion is a development of the general point above: let's bring together orthodox research and the happiness themes in this book – even when it's not initially obvious that happiness is involved. Much psychological research addresses happiness in terms that are feature-specific – positive or negative feelings about a particular activity, person, thing or idea. For instance, stressful aspects of an environment can give rise to feature-specific unhappiness in the form of strain in particular settings, and the characteristics, causes and consequences of strain can helpfully be viewed in the present terms. The book can also contribute to topics like motivation (think of goals and values) and learning (think of reinforcement and habits), as well as to studies of personality, ageing, social influence, attitudes, leadership and many themes in the subdisciplines of educational psychology, work psychology, cognitive psychology and clinical psychology. Please look into that possibility: how might your principal interests make use of some themes presented here, even if you had not previously recognized that you were studying happiness?

Examine together environmental and personal features

Publications about the correlates of wellbeing have typically focussed only on its associations with features of a situation or only on its associations with personal characteristics – to the exclusion of the other category of variable. There is a shortage of research that investigates external variables in combination with those from within the person, and more studies into both the environment and the person are now essential. As outlined in Chapter 5, significant increments from combined inputs have been found in some cases but not in others, and fresh models are needed about the characteristics that differentiate between the presence and the absence of significant person-environment combination.

Given that a standard level of environment-versus-person importance is not expected, moderators of the association between environmental features and wellbeing require particular attention. For instance, we need to develop thinking about the impact of situational strength (see Chapter 5) – some inputs from the environment are more powerful than others. And associations between the same situational feature and people's wellbeing can depend on which form of wellbeing is being studied. Increased understanding of those differences requires deeper understanding of the nature of wellbeing and the occurrence of conceptual overlap between situational aspects and associated feelings (again, see Chapter 5).

Investigate habits and other underlying constructs

Conceptual inquiries are also required to learn about factors that might underlie observed associations with happiness. For instance, some significant correlations between wellbeing and personality traits seem likely to derive in part from the fact that each trait is made up of a network of habits and the same habits might be implicated in happiness. The dispositional underpinnings of habitual behaviour require attention.

Habitual responses, their acquisition through learning and their role in motivation were central to much Western psychology throughout the 1930s and 1940s, but have more recently failed to attract much interest. Yet habits are everywhere: our lives substantially consist of them as we draw on routines from our mental autopilot. Those automatic routines concern thoughts and feelings as well as overt actions, and they extend across time and between situations. Habitual routines need to be reinstated within contemporary research. For instance, habit-change is central to the modification of psychologically harmful behaviours and thoughts: what are its principal processes?

In order to move forward in this area, it's essential to better conceptualize the operation of habits. In outline terms, they comprise sequences of cue, routine and reward, which have become largely automatic as a cue triggers behavioural or mental routines in anticipation of a specific reward.[6] Although a particular sequence of that kind might originally have been consciously created, its operation can become relatively fixed after being repeated – perhaps for hundreds of times across several years. As people seeking to diet[7] or break an addiction can confirm, disruption of these entrenched sequences is not straightforward. Research into habitual forms of thinking and feeling needs additional attention and development.

Examine the construct of wellbeing

We also need to develop our understanding of subjective wellbeing. Happiness researchers have traditionally studied hedonic indicators like life satisfaction, strain and burnout, and it would be useful also to examine aspects additional to and within those constructs. For instance, Chapter 3 has emphasized the importance of eudaimonic happiness, described here in terms of flourishing wellbeing. Happiness sources and consequences have very rarely been investigated in terms of flourishing, and those links should be included in future research. However, user-friendly measures of flourishing are so far underdeveloped, and additional questionnaire development is sorely needed.

Furthermore, conceptual and empirical work is needed to clarify how far flourishing and hedonic wellbeing can be treated as distinct and how they might be sequentially and causally interrelated. One possibility is that flourishing issues become personally salient only after hedonic happiness is reasonably acceptable, along the lines of Abraham Maslow's hierarchy of basic needs – physiological, safety, social, esteem and self-actualization.

Within hedonic happiness, we have seen in Chapter 2 that feelings differ in their degree of activation, illustrated in terms of positive wellbeing by the contrast between enthusiastic enjoyment and calm relaxation. Future studies need to discriminate between activation as well as valence, developing and testing hypotheses about feelings that differ in either way.

It is also desirable to learn about momentary and short-term wellbeing in addition to more extended life satisfaction, engagement and so on. For instance, how do feelings of wellbeing change in response to short-term shifts in conditions? How do environmental and personal factors contribute to wellbeing in the shorter term versus longer term? Diary studies, obtaining information at several times in the course of a day, are important here and have been developed in practical settings by several researchers.[8]

Create and apply measures of mental processes

Assessment of mental processes through introspective self-reports has become conventional in many areas of psychology – attitudes, motivation, personality traits, strain and so on. So it's certainly feasible to measure mental activity, and a more general shift in that direction is now desirable. In the area of this book, we need to create and assess self-report measures of feelings and thoughts in everyday activity. For example, value preferences for or against particular environmental features can easily be incorporated in studies of those features, and details of social or situational comparisons (Chapter 5) can readily be obtained. Straightforward questionnaire items about the themes of this book need to be developed and evaluated.

Explore clusters of contributing factors

Many studies investigate single variables that are likely to be supplemented by other variables. For instance, emotion regulation through emphasizing purposeful endeavours is important not only in its own right, but because it can lead onto the development of positive social relations and progress towards desirable goals. Similarly, particular values can operate within personality traits, so that combined trait-and-value investigations are sometimes called for. And hedonic adaptation is speeded or inhibited as a function of other processes in this book, such as reinterpreting a situation through new social comparisons or emphasizing a different set of counterfactual possibilities.

The traditional one-variable focus doesn't properly represent the multi-feature complexity that often occurs in reality. There is now a need to develop thinking about characteristic combinations of several mental processes and to incorporate compound-level indicators in studies that also examine constituent processes on their own. Linked studies should examine the conceptual and practical interdependence between situational features linked to happiness. For example, increased discretion (happiness-promoting feature 1) can lead to fewer guidelines about the kinds of behaviour that are appropriate and thus to a reduction in role clarity (feature 5).

Research of that kind raises issues about causal priority, for instance between longer-term characteristics and processes in a single situation. Modifying a situation (one form of emotion regulation) can bring about greater wellbeing, but situation-modifying behaviour is an instance of the general trait of proactivity, and that trait is itself empirically correlated with wellbeing. Should the greater wellbeing that can occur after modifying a situation be attributed to the particular activity or to the general trait of proactivity that in addition generates other potential contributors to wellbeing? Perhaps to both. How can theories be formulated in terms of both longer-term and shorter-term psychological variables?

Develop longitudinal and 'third-variable' research

Almost every study reviewed here has been cross-sectional, examining relationships at one point in time. Single-occasion investigations of that kind are essential to define key variables, describe a current reality, assess new measures, map out existing relationships and suggest causal possibilities, but they do not themselves uncover causality. Longitudinal investigations come closer to that, but (as we've seen in Chapter 6) even longitudinal findings are causally ambiguous.

Research needs to keep in mind unmeasured but possibly influential features – described earlier as 'third variables'. For instance, wellbeing is often studied as a function of one particular happiness-promoting feature from Chapter 4, although some of the other eight features could also be important. And in studying possible consequences of high or low happiness, prior happenings in an environment can be more influential than current happiness itself, but those prior events are typically omitted from a study.

Refine research into happiness-promoting activities

Chapter 6 described promising findings from experiments in which individuals apply procedures to increase their happiness – expressing gratitude, avoiding rumination and the like. Most of these studies were conducted with university students and followed them for only a few weeks, and key questions still have to be answered. For instance, if a self-help activity is found to be effective, how long do its happiness benefits last? How willing are people to stick with the activity across time? How frequently should someone apply it, since repeating the same effortful activity soon gets tedious? A common procedure is to ask for once-a-day application, but maybe a reduced frequency would be similarly effective. Or perhaps a mixture of different happiness-promoting activities would be more helpful. And research should also consider possible moderators: how do individual differences or situational features affect the outcomes of applying one of the self-help procedures?

Expand research into wellbeing interventions

Also needed are systematic studies of practical procedures to improve happiness in non-student samples, comparing outcomes against a control group. For instance, the programme for Promoting Adult Resilience has shown promise in several settings,[9] and there is considerable scope for the development and investigation of that and similar programmes.

Consider less orthodox forms of research

Some research issues could benefit from less conventional approaches. For example, the earlier suggestion to look simultaneously at environmental features and aspects of the person requires a relatively large sample and a broad spread of responses. Those can be difficult to obtain for many researchers, for example in a single setting, and alternative sources of data would often be helpful. Recent developments in the research use of internet sites[10] have created opportunities for obtaining large, targeted samples of volunteers, and the availability of online samples can provide a valuable impetus to person-and-environment studies of the kind emphasized here.

Most published research in this and associated fields has been from a quantitative perspective, analyzing numerical scores derived from a relatively large sample of people. Progress has been substantial, and quantitative research is likely to remain popular among academic psychologists. However, many issues require more intensive or discursive – qualitative – inquiries, and a great deal can be learned about happiness or unhappiness from interviews or targeted observations, perhaps accompanied by self-completion questionnaires and continuing across time. Qualitative psychological investigations are becoming increasingly sophisticated and popular[11] and should be given greater emphasis in research into happiness.

Apply the book's perspective to particular groups

Finally it's essential for themes of this book to be applied to particular sets of people, as in Chapter 4's consideration of three different groups – those who are unemployed, retired or homemaking. Additional groups are targeted in different subdisciplines of psychology, and researchers might develop themes and issues from the book within their own field. For example, educational psychologists might explore the nine happiness-promoting environmental characteristics among pupils or among schoolteachers. Work psychologists have created and tested specific models of job wellbeing that need to be developed through a more wide-ranging perspective. For clinical psychologists, there is considerable overlap between happiness and mental health. And cognitive psychologists can find in this book many issues that need their expertise; for instance, more sophisticated models of everyday habit formation and change are required.

This short book has necessarily described situations and processes in a general way, and that kind of broad perspective remains essential. But the current relatively abstract account needs to be supplemented by details in particular kinds of settings and with particular groups, and here the field of happiness depends on researchers across particular subdisciplines of psychology.

Research development: an overview

This section has drawn attention to 11 issues in need of more intensive psychological research. Different academic readers will have their own preferences and might wish to offer additional possibilities. From the standpoint of this book, the overarching need is for more psychologists to undertake more research into happiness in its different forms.

CHAPTER 7: SOME TAKE-HOME MESSAGES

As outlined in the first part of this chapter, it can be possible to improve your own happiness by examining your typical feelings, assessing your situation in the terms of this book and looking at your own characteristics and thought processes. The second section of the chapter is of more specialized interest, addressed to researchers and students of psychology. Within an overarching need for more research in this field, it's desirable to develop theories and empirical studies in the 11 areas outlined in this section.

NOTES ABOUT THE TEXT AND SOME ADDITIONAL READING

CHAPTER 1. AN INITIAL LOOK

1 For clarity of presentation, the abbreviation 'happiness' will often be used rather than the cumbersome 'happiness and unhappiness'.

2 Academic presentations along the current lines include those by Warr (1987, 2007, 2017); and a parallel account for the general reader is by Warr and Clapperton (2010). Research-based practical suggestions have been provided by Ben-Shahar (2007) and Lyubomirsky (2007). Many studies that emphasize specific models and detailed statistical relationships are illustrated in publications cited throughout the text.

3 See Oishi et al. (2013).

4 Of course, to some extent you can create your own good luck, for instance, by choosing to move into situations that might be good for you.

5 Uchida and Kitiyama (2009).

6 For instance, Mogilner et al. (2011).

7 The target of happiness can be a current situation or idea, or it may be imagined in the future or recalled from the past.

8 See, for example, Osgood et al. (1967).

9 These three levels of scope are positively intercorrelated, but influences on them can differ between levels. For instance, your bosses' behaviour can be more important in respect of your job satisfaction than it is for global satisfaction with life as a whole.

10 In addition, politicians and governments in several countries have recently expressed interest in projects to assess national wellbeing in parallel with economic indices of success.

11 Even people who are generally extremely happy experience unhappiness from time to time.

12 Recent discussions by psychologists in this field include those by Huta and Waterman (2014); Keyes et al. (2002); Seligman (2011, 2018); Ryff and Singer (2008); and Waterman (2008).

13 Publications in those terms by Maslow (e.g., 1954, 1973) and Herzberg (e.g., 1966) were very influential with the general public in previous decades, although they were not taken up by academic researchers. Maslow argued for a hierarchy of needs ranging upward from those that were physiological and safety-oriented through belongingness and esteem to processes of self-actualization; he believed that, in general, lower-level needs had to be attained before others became relevant.

14 Kahneman and Krueger (2006) have drawn attention to possible influences on extended recall, and described research showing that overall assessment of an entire period can place excessive weight on peak experiences and those occurring at the end of a specified period.

15 This perspective derives much from early thinking by Marie Jahoda (1958) and Carol Ryff (1989, 2014), and the framework outlined here has been covered in greater detail by Warr (1987).

CHAPTER 2. HEDONIC WELLBEING: FEELING BAD TO FEELING GOOD

1 Since the eighteenth century, cognition and affect (roughly, thought and feeling) have been two of the essential foundations of psychology. Studies of cognition examine, for instance, perception, memory, attention, reasoning and problem-solving – and affect has been explored in terms of emotions, moods, preferences and other kinds of personal evaluation.

2 This and many other scales provide seven options for each item from *strongly disagree* to *strongly agree*. See Diener et al. (1985) and Pavot and Diener (2008). Life satisfaction has also been studied through single items, such as 'Overall, I am satisfied with my life'.

3 Goldberg and Williams (1988).

4 Brayfield and Rothe (1951).

5 Ironson et al. (1989).

6 Russell (2003), p. 148.

7 Emotions and moods overlap with each other in the presence of affect but otherwise differ in several ways. For example, affect is generally viewed as within an emotion when it's relatively short term and can be placed in a defined category such as fear, anger or guilt. On the other hand, moods are typically more diffuse and of longer duration.

8 Based, for example, on Remington et al. (2000), Russell (1980, 2003) and Yik et al. (2011).

9 Russell (2003), p. 156.

10 As used here, the quadrant labels Anxiety and Depression are shorthand descriptors for sets of feelings; they do not denote the entirety of clinical conditions identified as 'Anxiety' and 'Depression'. Self-report questionnaires to record feelings in the four quadrants have been published by Burke et al. (1989), Van Katwyk et al. (2000), Warr (1990) and Warr et al. (2014).

11 For instance, Bakker and Oerlemans (2011) and Hakanen et al. (2018).

CHAPTER 3. FLOURISHING WELLBEING: SELF-WORTH AND A GOOD LIFE

1 Waterman (1993).

2 Ryff (1989), p. 1071.

3 Ryff used the label *psychological* wellbeing as a counter to *subjective* wellbeing, a conventional term for hedonic happiness.

4 Ryff (1989, 2014).

5 Peterson et al. (2005) and Seligman (2002, 2011).

6 Ryan and Deci (2001) and Ryan et al. (2008).

7 Ancient Greek and more recent philosophers have debated whether assessed worth should derive from some objective standard or be based only on subjective judgements of value. Different emphases have similarly occurred in psychologists' accounts of flourishing.

8 McGregor and Little (1998).

9 Seligman (2011), p. 12.

10 Baumeister et al. (2013) and King et al. (2006).

11 Czikszentmihalyi (1990, 2014), Moneta (2004) and subsequent papers in that symposium.

12 For example, see Keyes (2002) and Porath et al. (2012).

13 For instance, 'The most animating occasions of human life are calls to danger and hardship, not invitations to safety and ease' (Ferguson, 1767/1966, p. 45).

14 Waterman et al. (2010).

15 People can respond with varying degrees of agreement or disagreement. In this questionnaire, five response options are provided, from *strongly disagree* (scored 0) to *strongly agree* (scored 4).

16 Schutte et al. (2013) and Areepattamannil and Hashim (2017).

17 Diener et al. (2010).

18 With responses from Strongly Disagree to Strongly Agree, here with seven alternatives.

19 Hone et al. (2014) and Singh et al. (2016).

20 Steger et al. (2006).

21 Steger et al. (2012).

22 Su et al. (2014).

23 Five response options range from Strongly Disagree (scored 1) to Strongly Agree (scored 5).

24 Porath et al. (2012).

25 Ryan and Frederick (1997). Subsequent studies of the scale's validity include that by Bostic et al. (2000).

26 Ryff (1989), p. 1079.

27 For example, Compton et al. (1996), Keyes et al. (2002) and Goodman et al. (2018).

28 Disabato et al. (2016), p. 477.

29 See Seligman (2018).

CHAPTER 4. INFLUENCES FROM THE WORLD AROUND YOU: NINE PRINCIPAL FEATURES

1 For example, see Yeniaras and Akarsu (2017). The association is strongest among older people.

2 Ryff (2014).

3 For example, see Haushofer and Fehr (2014).

4 Warr (2018).

5 For example, see Warr (2007).

6 Up-and-down examples in these two paragraphs have been detailed in job settings by Warr (2007). Note that empirical tests require samples that

extend fully across the range of a job-feature possibility; in practice, adequate wide-range samples can be difficult to obtain, and some studies are less than ideal in terms of variance.

7 For example, a nation-level study by Jebb et al. (2018) examined wellbeing patterns in nine regions of the world. They found it usual for happiness to level off at moderate incomes and that in a minority of regions a very high income was accompanied by happiness reduction.

8 Research evidence and conceptual implications of the Vitamin Model in respect of happiness and unhappiness are discussed in more detail by Warr (2007). A briefer account can be found in the same author's chapter 'Environmental "vitamins", personal judgements, work values, and happiness' in S. Cartwright and C. L. Cooper (Eds.), *The Oxford handbook of organizational wellbeing*. Oxford: Oxford University Press, 2009.

9 Clark (2003), p. 326.

10 An often-unnoticed value of a paid job is its provision of structure to the day. After retirement, the lack of time-markers to break up experiences across many hours can be disheartening.

11 See, for instance, Klumb and Lampert (2004).

12 The Vitamin Model in jobs has been reviewed for non-academic readers by Warr and Clapperton (2010).

CHAPTER 5. INFLUENCES FROM WITHIN YOURSELF

1 See Bartels (2015), Bartels and Boomsma (2009) and Weiss et al. (2008).

2 This pattern has been shown for global (context-free) wellbeing and different forms of job happiness. See, for example, Cheng et al. (2017), Clark et al. (1996) and Steptoe et al. (2015).

3 Ryff (2014) and Ryff and Singer (2008).

4 See the lifespan model presented by Scheibe and Zacher (2013).

5 Nolen-Hoeksema and Rusting (1999) and Rosenfield and Mouzon (2013).

6 See, for example, Judge and Hulin (1993) and Eschleman and Bowling (2011).

7 When describing a dimension of personality, 'neuroticism' refers to a particular style of behaviour and outlook rather than to a medical condition. High scorers on personality scales of Neuroticism are not necessarily medically ill.

8 See, for example, Steel et al. (2008).

9   For example, Steel et al. (2008) and Lucas and Diener (2015).

10 The two components of Conscientiousness were studied separately by Inceoglu and Warr (2011), who found that the achievement-oriented subscale was particularly associated with job engagement.

11 Carver et al. (2010).

12 See, for example, Tornau and Frese (2013).

13 Ryff (2014).

14 For instance, Rokeach (1973) and Schwartz et al. (2000).

15 See, for example, Loher et al. (1985).

16 Luhmann et al. (2012).

17 Griffin (1988, 1991).

18 Boswell et al. (2005).

19 Headey and Wearing (1992).

20 For example, Cummins et al. (2014).

21 See also Gross (2014, 2015) and Quoidbach et al. (2015).

22 Other models of emotion regulation, such as that by Buruck et al. (2016), also extend across several of the stages considered here.

23 See, for example, Clauss et al. (2018), Lyubomirsky (2007) and Lyubomirsky and Layous (2013).

24 Sonnentag et al. (2010).

25 For example, Wheeler (2000).

26 For instance, Mair (2018).

27 Medvec et al. (1995).

28 Clark and Oswald (1996).

29 Quoidbach et al. (2015), p. 678.

30 Bond and Bunce (2003).

31 Kuba and Scheibe (2017).

32 Gross and John (2003).

33 For instance, Grandey (2015) and Hülsheger and Schewe (2011).

34 Treatments of appraisal and reappraisal have often been based on the earlier perspective of Lazarus and Folkman (1984).

35 Kuba and Scheibe (2017) and Scheibe and Zacher (2013).

36 For instance, Wheeler (2000).

37 Rudolph et al. (2017).

38 For example, Mischel (1977).

39 Bowling et al. (2015) and Warr and Inceoglu (2015).

CHAPTER 6. SOME CONSEQUENCES OF HAPPINESS

1 Studies of possible consequences have all focused on hedonic rather than flourishing happiness.
2 Lyubomirsky et al. (2005).
3 See Kraus (1995). Later analyses of this kind have examined a restricted subset of attitudes or behaviours; they all find strong positive correlations, as in the 1995 review.
4 Occupational research of this kind has been summarized by Warr and Nielsen (2018).
5 See, for instance, Riketta (2008). The magnitude of a lagged correlation declines with increases in interval between the two measurements.
6 See, for example, Forgas (2001), Forgas and George (2001) and Isen (1999).
7 Oswald et al. (2015).
8 For example, Seo et al. (2004).
9 For example, Bowling et al. (2015).
10 As expected by George and Brief (1992) and found by Warr et al. (2014).
11 Baas et al. (2008) and Warr et al. (2014).
12 Some readers will have noticed that this chapter's concern for causal proof was not paralleled in Chapter 4, when environmental features were discussed as sources of happiness. Correlational evidence in that chapter is also causally ambiguous, but our personal experience and repeated occurrences have encouraged causal conclusions.
13 Comprehensive reviews of this field are by Diener and Chan (2011), Diener et al. (2017) and Pressman and Cohen (2005).
14 Kim et al. (2016).
15 Diener et al. (2017), p. 140.
16 Diener and Chan (2011), p. 8.

CHAPTER 7. WHAT TO DO NOW?

1 Feelings, of course, vary in degree in each of these ways.
2 In practice, the two often go together.
3 See Ben-Shahar (2007), p 109. He presents a video introduction at www. happier.tv/playlist/423/introducing-happiness.

4   See, for example, the website www.authentichappiness.org.

5   Lyubomirsky (2007).

6   This point has been developed for general readers by business journalist Charles Duhigg (2013). More academic perspectives are by Gardner (2015) and Wood and Rünger (2016).

7   See, for example Ogden (2018).

8   For example, see Sonnentag (2015).

9   One comparison is by Foster et al. (2018).

10 See, for example, Gosling and Mason (2015) and Hewson et al. (2016).

11 For example, see Symon and Cassell (2012) and Pratt and Bonaccio (2016).

REFERENCES CITED IN THE TEXT

Areepattamannil, S., & Hashim, J. (2017). The questionnaire for Eudaimonic Well-Being (QEWB): Psychometric properties in a non-western adolescent sample. *Personality and Individual Differences, 117*, 236–241.

Baas, M., De Dreu, C. K. W., & Nijstad, B. A. (2008). A meta-analysis of 25 years of mood-creativity research: Hedonic tone, activation, or regulatory focus? *Psychological Bulletin, 134*, 779–806.

Bakker, A. B., & Oerlemans, W. G. M. (2011). Subjective well-being in organizations. In K. Cameron and G. Spreitzer (Eds.), *Handbook of positive organizational scholarship* (pp. 178–189). Oxford: Oxford University Press.

Bartels, M. (2015). Genetics of wellbeing and its components satisfaction with life, happiness, and quality of life: A review and meta-analysis of heritability studies. *Behavior Genetics, 45*, 137–156.

Bartels, M., & Boomsma, D. I. (2009). Born to be happy? The etiology of subjective well-being. *Behavior Genetics, 39*, 605–615.

Baumeister, R. F., Vohs, K. D., Aaker, J. L, & Garbinsky, E. N. (2013). Some key differences between a happy life and a meaningful life. *Journal of Positive Psychology, 8*, 505–516.

Ben-Shahar, T. (2007). *Happier*. New York, NY: McGraw-Hill.

Bond, F. W., & Bunce, D. (2003). The role of acceptance and job control in mental health, job satisfaction, and work performance. *Journal of Applied Psychology, 88*, 1057–1067.

Bostic, T. J., Rubio, D. M., & Hood, M. (2000). A validation of the subjective vitality scale using structural equation modeling. *Social Indicators Research*, 52, 313–324.

Boswell, W. R., Boudreau, J. W., & Tichy, J. (2005). The relationship between employee job change and job satisfaction: The honeymoon-hangover effect. *Journal of Applied Psychology*, 90, 882–892.

Bowling, N. A., Khazon, S., Meyer, R. M., & Burrus, C. J. (2015). Situational strength as a moderator of the relationship between job satisfaction and job performance. *Journal of Business and Psychology*, 30, 89–104.

Brayfield, A. H., & Rothe, H. F. (1951). An index of job satisfaction. *Journal of Applied Psychology*, 35, 307–311.

Burke, M. J., Brief, A. P., George, J. M., Roberson, L., & Webster, J. (1989). Measuring affect at work: Confirmatory analyses of competing mood structures with conceptual linkage to cortical regulatory systems. *Journal of Personality and Social Psychology*, 57, 1091–1102.

Buruck, G., Dörfel, D., Kugler, J., & Brom, S. S. (2016). Enhancing well-being at work: The role of emotion regulation skills as personal resources. *Journal of Occupational Health Psychology*, 21, 480–493.

Carver, C. S., Scheier, M. F., & Segerstrom, S. C. (2010). Optimism. *Clinical Psychology Review*, 30, 879–889.

Cheng, T. C., Powdthavee, N., & Oswald, A. J. (2017). Longitudinal evidence for a midlife nadir in human well-being: Results from four data-sets. *The Economic Journal*, 127, 126–142.

Clark, A. E. (2003). Unemployment as a social norm: Psychological evidence from panel data. *Journal of Labor Economics*, 21, 323–351.

Clark, A. E., & Oswald, A. J. (1996). Satisfaction and comparison income. *Journal of Public Economics*, 61, 359–381.

Clark, A. E., Oswald, A., & Warr, P. B. (1996). Is job satisfaction U-shaped in age? *Journal of Occupational and Organizational Psychology*, 69, 57–81.

Clauss, E., Hoppe, A., O'Shea, D., Gonzáles Morales, M. G., Steidle, A., & Michel, A. (2018). Promoting personal resources and reducing exhaustion through positive work reflection among caregivers. *Journal of Occupational Health Psychology*, 23, 127–140.

Compton, W. C., Smith, M. L., Cornish, K. A., & Qualls D. L. (1996). Factor structure of mental health measures. *Journal of Personality and Social psychology*, 71, 406–413.

Cummins, R. A., Li, N., Wooden, M., & Stokes, M. (2014). A demonstration of set-points for subjective wellbeing. *Journal of Happiness Studies*, 15, 183–206.

Czikszentmihalyi, M. (1990). *Flow*. New York, NY: Harper and Row.

Czikszentmihalyi, M. (2014). *Flow and the foundations of positive psychology: The collected works of Mihaly Csikszentmihalyi*. New York, NY: Springer.

Diener, E., & Chan, M. Y. (2011). Happy people live longer: Subjective well-being contributes to health and longevity. *Applied Psychology: Health and Well-Being*, 3, 1–43.

Diener, E., Emmons, R. A., Larsen, R. J., & Griffin, S. (1985). The satisfaction with life scale. *Journal of Personality Assessment*, 49, 71–75.

Diener, E., Pressman, S., Hunter, J., & Chase, D. (2017). If, why, and when subjective well-being influences health, and future needed research. *Applied Psychology: Health and Well-Being*, 9, 133–167.

Diener, E., Wirtz, D., Tov, W., Kim-Prieto, C., Choi, D, Oishi, S., & Biswas-Diener, R. (2010). New well-being measures: Short scales to assess flourishing and positive and negative feelings. *Social Indicators Research*, 97, 143–156.

Disabato, D. J., Goodman, F. R., Kashdan, T. B., Short, J. L., & Jarden, A. (2016). Different types of well-being? A cross-cultural examination of Hedonic and Eudaimonic well-being. *Psychological Assessment*, 28, 471–482.

Duhigg, C. (2013). *The power of habit*. London: Random House.

Eschleman, K. J., & Bowling, N. A. (2011). A construct validation of the neutral objects satisfaction questionnaire. *Journal of Business and Psychology*, 26, 501–515.

Ferguson, A. (1767/1966). *An essay on the history of civil society*. Edinburgh, UK: Edinburgh University Press.

Forgas, J. P. (Ed.) (2001). *Handbook of affect and social cognition*. Mahwah, NJ: Erlbaum.

Forgas, J. P., & George, J. M. (2001). Affective influences on judgments and behavior in organizations. *Organizational Behavior and Human Decision Processes*, 86, 3–34.

Foster, K., Shocket, I., Wurfl, A., Roche, M., Maybery, D., Shakespeare-Finch, J., & Furness, T. (2018). On PAR: A feasibility study of the Promoting Adult Resilience programme with mental health nurses. *International Journal of Mental Health Nursing*, 27, 1470–1480.

Gardner, B. (2015). A review and analysis of the use of 'habit' in understanding, predicting and influencing health-related behaviour. *Health Psychology Review*, 9, 277–295.

George, J. M., & Brief, A. P. (1992). Feeling good-doing good: A conceptual analysis of the mood at work-organizational spontaneity relationship. *Psychological Bulletin, 112,* 310–329.

Goldberg, D. P., & Williams, P. (1988). *A user's guide to the general health questionnaire.* Windsor, UK: NFER-Nelson.

Goodman, F. R., Disabato, D. J., Kashdan, T. B., & Kauffman, S. B. (2018). Measuring well-being: A comparison of subjective well-being and PERMA. *Journal of Positive Psychology, 13,* 321–332.

Gosling, S. D., & Mason, W. (2015). Internet research in psychology. *Annual Review of Psychology, 66,* 877–902.

Grandey, A. A. (2015). Smiling for a wage: What emotional labor teaches us about emotion regulation. *Psychological Inquiry, 26,* 54–60.

Griffin, R. W. (1988). Consequences of quality circles in an industrial setting: A longitudinal assessment. *Academy of Management Journal, 31,* 338–358.

Griffin, R. W. (1991). Effects of work redesign on employee perceptions, attitudes, and behaviors: A long-term investigation. *Academy of Management Journal, 34,* 425–435.

Gross, J. J. (1998). The emerging field of emotion regulation: An integrative review. *Review of General Psychology, 2,* 271–299.

Gross, J. J. (Ed.) (2014). *Handbook of emotion regulation,* second edition. New York, NY: Guilford Press.

Gross, J. J. (2015). Emotion regulation: Current status and future perspectives. *Psychological Inquiry, 26,* 1–26.

Gross, J. J., & John, O. P. (2003). Individual differences in emotion regulation processes: Implications for affect, relationships, and well-being. *Journal of Personality and Social Psychology, 85,* 348–362.

Hakanen, J. J., Peeters, M. C. W., & Schaufeli, W. B. (2018). Different types of employee well-being across time and their relationships with job crafting. *Journal of Occupational Health Psychology, 23,* 289–301.

Haushofer, J., & Fehr, E. (2014). On the psychology of poverty. *Science, 344,* 862–867.

Headey, B., & Wearing, A. (1992). *Understanding happiness: A theory of subjective well-being.* Melbourne: Longman Cheshire.

Herzberg, F. (1966). *Work and the nature of man.* Chicago, IL: World Publishing.

Hewson, C., Vogel, C., & Laurent, D. (2016). *Internet research methods.* London: Sage.

Hone, L., Jarden, A., & Schofield, G. (2014). Psychometric properties of the flourishing scale in a New Zealand sample. *Social Indicators Research*, 119, 1031–1045.

Hülsheger, U. R., & Schewe, A. F. (2011). On the costs and benefits of emotional labor: A meta-analysis of three decades of research. *Journal of Occupational Health Psychology*, 16, 361–389.

Huta, V., & Waterman, A. S. (2014). Eudaimonia and its distinction from hedonia: Developing a classification and terminology for understanding conceptual and operational definitions. *Journal of Happiness Studies*, 15, 1425–1456.

Inceoglu, I., & Warr, P. (2011). Personality and job engagement. *Journal of Personnel Psychology*, 10, 177–181.

Ironson, G. H., Smith, P. C., Brannick, M. T., Gibson, W. M., & Paul, K. B. (1989). Construction of a job in general scale: A comparison of global, composite, and specific measures. *Journal of Applied Psychology*, 74, 193–200.

Isen, A. M. (1999). Positive affect. In T. Dagleish and M. Power (Eds.), *Handbook of cognition and emotion* (pp. 521–539). New York, NY: Wiley.

Jahoda, M. (1958). *Current concepts of positive mental health*. New York, NY: Basic Books.

Jebb, A. T., Tay, L., Diener, E., & Oishi, S. (2018). Happiness, income satiation and turning points around the world. *Nature Human Behaviour*, 2, 33–38.

Judge, T. A., & Hulin, C. L. (1993). Job satisfaction as a reflection of disposition: A multiple source causal analysis. *Organizational Behavior and Human Decision Processes*, 56, 388–421.

Kahneman, D., & Krueger, A. B. (2006). Developments in the measurement of subjective well-being. *Journal of Economic Perspectives*, 20, 3–24.

Keyes, C. L. M. (2002). The mental health continuum: From languishing to flourishing in life. *Journal of Health and Social Behavior*, 43, 207–222.

Keyes, C. L. M., Schmotkin, D., & Ryff, C. D. (2002). Optimizing well-being: The empirical encounter of two traditions. *Journal of Personality and Social Psychology*, 82, 1007–1022.

Kim, E. S., Hagan, K. A., Grodstein, F., DeMeo, D. L., De Vivo, I., & Kubzansky, L. D. (2016). Optimism and cause-specific mortality: A prospective cohort study. *American Journal of Epidemiology*, 185, 21–29.

King, L. A., Hicks, J. A., Krull, J. L., & Del Gaiso, A. K. (2006). Positive affect and the experience of meaning in life. *Journal of Personality and Social Psychology*, 90, 179–196.

Klumb, P. L., & Lampert, T. (2004). Women, work, and well-being 1950–2000: A review and methodological critique. *Social Science and Medicine, 58*, 1007–1024.

Kraus, S. J. (1995). Attitudes and the prediction of behavior: A meta-analysis of the empirical literature. *Personality and Social Psychology Bulletin, 21*, 58–75.

Kuba, K., & Scheibe, S. (2017). Let it be and keep on going! Acceptance and daily occupational well-being in relation to negative work events. *Journal of Occupational Health Psychology, 22*, 59–70.

Lazarus, R. S., & Folkman, S. (1984). *Stress, appraisal, and coping.* New York: Springer.

Loher, B. T., Noe, R. A., Moeller, N. L., & Fitzgerald, M. P. (1985). A meta-analysis of the relation of job characteristics to job satisfaction. *Journal of Applied Psychology, 70*, 280–289.

Lucas, R. E., & Diener, E. (2015). Personality and subjective well-being: Current issues and controversies. In M. Mikulincer and P. R. Shaver (Eds.), *APA handbook of personality and social psychology* (pp. 577–599). Washington, DC: American Psychological Association.

Luhmann, M., Hofmann, W., Eid, M., & Lucas, R. E. (2012). Subjective well-being and adaptation to life events: A meta-analysis. *Journal of Personality and Social Psychology, 102*, 592–615.

Lyubomirsky, S. (2007). *The how of happiness.* London: Littlebrown Group.

Lyubomirsky, S. (2013). *The myths of happiness.* New York, NY: Penguin Books.

Lyubomirsky, S., King, L., & Diener, E. (2005). The benefits of frequent positive affect: Does happiness lead to success? *Psychological Bulletin, 131*, 803–855.

Lyubomirsky, S., & Layous, K. (2013). How do simple positive activities increase well-being? *Current Directions in Psychological Science, 22*, 57–62.

Mair, C. (2018). *The psychology of fashion.* Abingdon, UK and New York, NY: Routledge.

Maslow, A. H. (1954). *Motivation and personality.* New York, NY: Harper and Row.

Maslow, A. H. (1973). *The farther reaches of human nature.* Harmondsworth: Penguin Books.

McGregor, I., & Little, B. R. (1998). Personal projects, happiness, and meaning: On doing well and being yourself. *Journal of Personality and Social Psychology, 74*, 494–512.

Medvec, V. H., Madey, S. F., & Gilovich, T. (1995). When less is more: Counterfactual thinking and satisfaction among Olympic Athletes. *Journal of Personality and Social Psychology, 69*, 603–610.

Mischel, W. (1977). The interaction of person and situation. In D. Magnusson and N. S. Endler (Eds.), *Personality at the cross-roads* (pp. 333–352). Hillsdale, NJ: Erlbaum.

Mogilner, C., Kamvar, S. D., & Aaker, J. (2011). The shifting meaning of happiness. *Social Psychological and Personality Science, 2,* 395–402.

Moneta, G. B. (2004). The flow experience across cultures. *Journal of Happiness Studies, 5,* 115–121.

Nolen-Hoeksema, S., & Rusting, C. (1999). Gender differences in well-being. In D. Kahneman, E. Diener, & N. Schwarz (Eds.), *Well-being: The foundations of hedonic psychology* (pp. 330–350). New York, NY: Russell Sage Foundation.

Ogden, J. (2018). *The psychology of dieting.* Abingdon, UK: Routledge.

Oishi, S., Graham, J., Kesebir, S., & Galinha, I. C. (2013). Concepts of happiness across time and cultures. *Personality and Social Psychology Bulletin, 39,* 559–577.

Osgood, C. E., Suci, G. C., & Tannenbaum, P. (1967). *The measurement of meaning.* Urbana, IL: University of Illinois Press.

Oswald, A. J., Proto, E., & Sgroi, D. (2015). Happiness and productivity. *Journal of Labor Economics, 33,* 789–822.

Pavot, W., & Diener, E. (2008). The satisfaction with life scale and the emerging construct of life satisfaction. *Journal of Positive Psychology, 3,* 137–152.

Peterson, C., Park, N., & Seligman, M. E. P. (2005). Orientations to happiness, and life satisfaction: The full life versus the empty life. *Journal of Happiness Studies, 6,* 25–41.

Porath, C., Spreitzer, G., Gibson, C., & Garnett, F. G. (2012). Thriving at work: Toward its measurement, construct validation, and theoretical refinement. *Journal of Organizational Behavior, 33,* 250–275.

Pratt, M. G., & Bonaccio, S. (2016). Qualitative research in I-O psychology: Maps, myths, and moving forward. *Industrial and Organizational Psychology, 9,* 693–715.

Pressman, S. D., & Cohen, S. (2005). Does positive affect influence health? *Psychological Bulletin, 131,* 925–971.

Quoidbach, J., Mikolajczak, M., & Gross, J. J. (2015). Positive interventions: An emotion regulation perspective. *Psychological Bulletin, 141,* 655–693.

Remington, N. A., Fabrigar, L. R., & Visser, P. S. (2000). Re-examining the circumplex model of affect. *Journal of Personality and Social Psychology, 79,* 286–300.

Riketta, M. (2008). The causal relation between job attitudes and performance: A meta-analysis of panel studies. *Journal of Applied Psychology, 93,* 472–481.

Rokeach, M. (1973). *The nature of human values*. New York, NY: Collier Macmillan.

Rosenfield, S., & Mouzon, D. (2013). Gender and mental health. In C. S. Aneshensel, J. C. Phelan, and A. Bierman (Eds.), *Handbook of the sociology of mental health* (pp. 277–296). Dordrecht, Netherlands: Springer.

Rudolph, C. W., Katz, I. M., Lavigne, K. N., & Zacher, H. (2017). Job crafting: A meta-analysis of relationships with individual differences, job characteristics, and work outcomes. *Journal of Vocational Behavior, 102*, 112–138.

Russell, J. A. (1980). A circumplex model of affect. *Journal of Personality and Social Psychology, 39*, 1161–1178.

Russell, J. A. (2003). Core affect and the psychological construction of emotion. *Psychological Review, 110*, 145–172.

Ryan, R. M., & Deci, E. L. (2001). On happiness and human potentials: A review of research on Hedonic and Eudaimonic well-being. *Annual Review of Psychology, 52*, 141–166.

Ryan, R. M., & Frederick, C. M. (1997). On energy, personality and health: Subjective vitality as a dynamic reflection of well-being. *Journal of Personality, 65*, 529–565.

Ryan, R. M., Huta, V., & Deci, E. L. (2008). Living well: A self-determination perspective on eudaimonia. *Journal of Happiness Studies, 9*, 139–170.

Ryff, C. D. (1989). Happiness is everything, or is it? Explorations on the meaning of psychological well-being. *Journal of Personality and Social Psychology, 57*, 1069–1081.

Ryff, C. D. (2014). Psychological well-being revisited: Advances in science and practice. *Psychotherapy and Psychosomatics, 83*, 10–28.

Ryff, C. D., & Singer, B. H. (2008). Know thyself and become what you are: A Eudaimonic approach to psychological well-being. *Journal of Happiness Studies, 9*, 13–39.

Scheibe, S., & Zacher, H. (2013). A lifespan perspective on emotion regulation and well-being in the workplace. *Research in Occupational Stress and Well-Being, 11*, 163–193.

Schutte, L., Wissing, M. P., & Kumalo, I. P. (2013). Further validation of the Questionnaire for Eudaimonic Well-Being (QEWB). *Psychology of Well-Being: Research and Practice, 3*, 3.

Schwartz, S. H., Sagiv, L., & Boehnke, K. (2000). Worries and values. *Journal of Personality, 68*, 309–346.

Seligman, M. E. P. (2002). *Authentic happiness.* New York, NY: Free Press.

Seligman, M. E. P. (2011). *Flourish.* New York, NY: Free Press.

Seligman, M. E. P. (2018). PERMA and the building blocks of well-being. Journal of *Positive Psychology*, 13, 333–335.

Seo, M. G., Feldman Barrett, L., & Bartunek, J. M. (2004). The role of affective experience in work motivation. *Academy of Management Review*, 29, 423–439.

Singh, K., Junnarkar, M., & Jaswal, S. (2016). Validating the flourishing scale and the scale of positive and negative experience in India. *Mental Health, Religion and Culture*, 19, 943–954.

Sonnentag, S. (2015). Dynamics of well-being. *Annual Review of Organizational Psychology and Organizational Behavior*, 2, 261–293.

Sonnentag, S., Binnewies, C., & Mojza, E. J. (2010). Staying well and engaged when demands are high: The role of psychological detachment. *Journal of Applied Psychology*, 95, 965–976.

Steel, P., Schmidt, J., & Schultz, J. (2008). Refining the relationship between personality and subjective well-being. *Psychological Bulletin*, 134, 138–161.

Steger, M. F., Dik, B. J., & Duffy, R. D. (2012). Measuring meaningful work: The Work and Meaning Inventory (WAMI). *Journal of Career Assessment*, 20, 322–337.

Steger, M. F., Frazier, P., Oishi, S., & Kaler, M. (2006). The meaning in life questionnaire: Assessing the presence of and search for meaning in life. *Journal of Counseling Psychology*, 53, 80–93.

Steptoe, A., Deaton, A., & Stone, A. A. (2015). Subjective well-being, health, and ageing. *The Lancet*, 385 (February 14), 640–648.

Su, R., Tay, L., & Diener, E. (2014). The development and validation of the Comprehensive Inventory of Thriving (CIT) and the Brief Inventory of Thriving (BIT). *Applied Psychology: Health and Well-Being*, 6, 251–279.

Symon, G., & Cassell, C. (2012). *Qualitative organizational research: Core methods and current challenges.* London: Sage.

Tornau, K., & Frese, M. (2013). Construct clean-up in proactivity research: A meta-analysis on the nomological net of work-related proactivity and their incremental validities. *Applied Psychology: An International Review*, 62, 44–96.

Uchida, Y., & Kitiyama, S. (2009). Happiness and unhappiness in East and West: Themes and variations. *Emotion*, 9, 441–456.

Van Katwyk, P. T., Fox, S. Spector, P. E., & Kelloway, E. K. (2000). Using the Job-related Affective Well-being Scale (JAWS) to investigate affective responses to work stressors. *Journal of Occupational Health Psychology*, 5, 219–230.

Warr, P. B. (1987). *Work, unemployment and mental health*. Oxford: Oxford University Press.

Warr, P. B. (1990). The measurement of well-being and other aspects of mental health. *Journal of Occupational Psychology*, 63, 193–210.

Warr, P. B. (2007). *Work, happiness, and unhappiness*. Mahwah, NJ: Erlbaum.

Warr, P. B. (2017). Happiness and mental health. In C. L. Cooper and J. C. Quick (Eds.), *The handbook of stress and health: A guide to research and practice* (pp. 57–74). London: Wiley.

Warr, P. B. (2018). Self-employment, personal values, and varieties of happiness-unhappiness. *Journal of Occupational Health Psychology*, 23, 388–401.

Warr, P. B., Bindl, U. K., Parker, S. K., & Inceoglu, I. (2014). Four-quadrant investigation of job-related affects and behaviours. *European Journal of Work and Organizational Psychology*, 23, 342–363.

Warr, P. B., & Clapperton, G. (2010). *The joy of work? Jobs, happiness, and you*. Abingdon: Routledge.

Warr, P. B., & Inceoglu, I. (2015). Job features, job values, and affective strength. *European Journal of Work and Organizational Psychology*, 24, 101–112.

Warr, P. B., & Nielsen, K. (2018). Wellbeing and work performance. In E. Diener, S. Oishi, and L. Tay (Eds.), *Handbook of well-being*. Salt Lake City, UT: DEF Publishers. Open access: https://nobascholar.com/books/1.

Waterman, A. S. (1993). Two conceptions of happiness: Contrasts of personal expressiveness (eudaimonia) and hedonic enjoyment. *Journal of Personality and Social Psychology*, 64, 678–691.

Waterman, A. S. (2008). Reconsidering happiness: A eudaimonist's perspective. *Journal of Positive Psychology*, 3, 234–252.

Waterman, A. S., Schwartz, S. J., Zamboanga, B. L., Ravert, R. D., Williams, M. K., Agocha, V. B., Kim, S. Y., & Donnellen, M. B. (2010). The questionnaire for eudaimonic well-being: Psychometric properties, demographic comparisons, and evidence of validity. *Journal of Positive Psychology*, 5, 41–61.

Weiss, A., Bates, T. C., & Luciano, M. (2008). Happiness is a personal(ity) thing. *Psychological Science*, 19, 205–210.

Wheeler, L. (2000). Individual differences in social comparison. In J. Suls and L. Wheeler (Eds.), *Handbook of social comparison: Theory and research* (pp. 141–158). New York, NY: Kluwer/Plenum.

Wood, W., & Rünger, D. (2016). Psychology of habit. *Annual Review of Psychology, 67,* 289–314.

Yeniaras, V., & Akarsu, T. N. (2017). Religiosity and life satisfaction: A multidimensional approach. *Journal of Happiness Studies, 18,* 1815–1840.

Yik, M., Russell, J. A., & Steiger, J. H. (2011). A 12-point circumplex structure of core affect. *Emotion, 11,* 705–711.

INDEX